# EDUCATOR OR BULLY?
## Managing the 21st-Century Classroom

Marie Menna Pagliaro

ROWMAN & LITTLEFIELD EDUCATION

A division of
ROWMAN & LITTLEFIELD PUBLISHERS, INC.
*Lanham • New York • Toronto • Plymouth, UK*

Published by Rowman & Littlefield Education
A division of Rowman & Littlefield Publishers, Inc.
A wholly owned subsidiary of The Rowman & Littlefield Publishing Group, Inc.
4501 Forbes Boulevard, Suite 200, Lanham, Maryland 20706
http://www.rowmaneducation.com

Estover Road, Plymouth PL6 7PY, United Kingdom

Copyright © 2011 by Marie Menna Pagliaro

*All rights reserved.* No part of this book may be reproduced in any form or by any electronic or mechanical means, including information storage and retrieval systems, without written permission from the publisher, except by a reviewer who may quote passages in a review.

British Library Cataloguing in Publication Information Available

**Library of Congress Cataloging-in-Publication Data**
Pagliaro, Marie Menna, 1934–
  Educator or bully? : managing the 21st century classroom / Marie Menna Pagliaro.
    p. cm.
  Includes bibliographical references.
  ISBN 978-1-61048-450-3 (cloth : alk. paper) — ISBN 978-1-61048-451-0 (pbk. : alk. paper) — ISBN 978-1-61048-452-7 (electronic)
  1. Classroom management—United States. 2. School discipline—United States. 3. Teacher-student relationships—United States. I. Title.
  LB3013.P245 2011
  371.102'40973—dc23                                                        2011022083

∞™ The paper used in this publication meets the minimum requirements of American National Standard for Information Sciences—Permanence of Paper for Printed Library Materials, ANSI/NISO Z39.48-1992.

Printed in the United States of America

# Contents

Introduction     v

## Part I: Guidelines for Improving Classroom Management

1. Societal Changes in the Twenty-First Century     3
2. Proactive Approaches to Classroom Management     11
3. Reactive Approaches to Classroom Management     35
4. Being Thorough When Considering Other Management Factors in Your Classroom     47
5. Maximizing Preparation for the Opening of School     51
6. Developing Professionally     61

## Part II: Reviewing/Acquiring Classroom Management Strategies (Systems)

7. The Necessity for Reviewing/Acquiring Specific Classroom Management Strategies     77
8. Teacher Effectiveness Training (T.E.T.)     81
9. Social Discipline     87
10. Reality Therapy     95
11. Assertive Discipline     103
12. Behavior Modification (Contingency Contracting)     109

References     117

About the Author     125

# Introduction

MOST TEACHERS ARE SHOCKED when they first read the question in the title of this book. Perhaps you had the same reaction. But teachers often resort to bullying tactics without realizing it.

Researchers have reported that teachers help standardize bullying when they either ignore it or engage in it themselves. For example, a teacher may humiliate a student in front of the class (Viadero, 2010).

Several school administrators have expressed concern recently over the difficulty they are having distinguishing between the behavior of students who are bullies and strategies teachers use in classroom management (Starr, 2003). Starr states that Harry Wong, an educational expert, has indicated that classroom management involves routines and procedures that foster the teacher's ability to teach and the students' ability to learn. Teachers who can teach, manage their classrooms. These teachers are educators. Teachers who can't teach, manage their students. These teachers are bullies.

In running any organization or production, such as corporations, cooking shows, plays, or operas, all factors have to be considered to ensure success. Classroom management is a similar venture. It is a comprehensive process that integrates all interdependent components—student knowledge, an engaging curriculum, robust instruction, developing students as responsible learners, and self-reflecting teachers (Hanson, 1998).

The most crucial component of classroom management is setting up an environment that makes instruction flow smoothly with minimal interruptions and student misbehaviors. This environment is the component with which this book is concerned.

Classroom management, the kind that organizes an orderly environment and promotes effective ways of handling student behavior, is one of the three most important skills a teacher can demonstrate (Marzano, 2003a). Not only is skill in managing a classroom a major factor in determining the success of a teacher (Brophy & Evertson, 1976), but in reviewing over 11,000 subsequent research studies, skill in classroom management was found to be *the* most important factor with respect to its effect on student achievement (Wang et al., 1993; Evertson & Weinstein, 2006).

Though you may believe that teaching academic subject matter should be your top priority, the reality is, "You will never be able to conduct instruction and effectively teach your class until you are able to manage the behavior of *all* [italics in original] of your students" (Canter, 2006, p. 123) with the goal of having them eventually manage themselves. Canter goes on to say that you will actually save academic teaching time as well as energy by putting management first.

This book offers a comprehensive approach to classroom management. The book was written for practicing teachers, both novice and veteran, who are interested in examining their current classroom management practices, especially with respect to how they reflect a twenty-first-century view. Student teachers will find the guidelines in this book valuable, as will college professors, who have consistently reported increasing classroom management problems in colleges and universities (Sternberg, 2010).

Since teachers are busy professionals, classroom management guidelines are presented clearly and succinctly. Examples of guidelines applicable to both elementary and secondary schools are offered, frequently contrasting traditional with contemporary approaches.

As professionals, teachers will want to be assured that their classroom management practice is based on sound theory and recent research. With the exception of references to seminal and foundational works upon which practice has been built and expanded, much of the supportive research provided is from the past decade.

In addition to teacher classroom management skills, there is a current emphasis on the responsibility the *student* should have in successful classroom management (Marzano, 2003b; McLeod et al., 2003). Since classroom management is not isolated from but should be an integral part of all school activities, there should be a building and even a district plan with a general consensus for managing classes. You could have a strong influence in establishing this plan, and will be in a better position to do so when you complete this book.

Part I covers the guidelines teachers can examine to deal with everyday classroom management interactions with a focus on twenty-first-century approaches. In this part there is an emphasis on preventive measures teachers can take followed by reactive procedures teachers can implement once problems have occurred.

Punishment and logical consequences are distinguished and the need for using educative techniques in handling misbehavior is emphasized. Part I concludes with a thorough consideration regarding how to organize and maintain the physical classroom environment and how to prepare for the beginning of school.

Questions for self-reflection follow at appropriate times so that teachers can examine their current practices and expand their repertoires to include more contemporary approaches. To ensure that this book provides the reader access to a comprehensive variety of ideas, when appropriate, contrary views are indicated.

Part II covers specific strategies (systems) teachers can use to deal with diverse classroom needs. These strategies range from the least intrusive and most student centered to those in which the teacher has more of the control.

In keeping with the attempt to offer contemporary approaches to classroom management, for each strategy that is more teacher controlled, suggestions are provided to make the student more involved and responsible. The foundational theory for each strategy is explained followed by the way that strategy can be implemented in the classroom. The teacher's belief system and personality are discussed along with the necessity to consider these when selecting strategies for implementation.

Knowledge becomes most powerful when it can be translated into performance. For teachers who are interested in improving their classroom management performance, coaching rubrics, unique to this book, are provided at relevant points. The coaching rubrics were developed collaboratively by teachers, professors, and teacher education students and have been field tested. These rubrics summarize the content and identify criteria for best practices. A rationale for rubrics and a detailed explanation regarding their use is presented.

While teachers can practice on their own using the coaching rubrics, it is more effective to practice and then obtain feedback on that performance from colleagues. This practice benefits not only the teacher but the teacher's peers as well.

Life will become less stressful as you progress in improving your classroom management skills. Good luck in your venture.

Marie Menna Pagliaro

# I
# GUIDELINES FOR IMPROVING CLASSROOM MANAGEMENT

# 1
# Societal Changes in the Twenty-First Century

THERE IS NO DOUBT THAT OUR SOCIETY is changing rapidly. Information continues to double every seventy-two hours and will be exploding even more quickly in the future (Jensen, 1998). Our classrooms are increasing in social, emotional, cultural, and academic diversity. Moreover, classrooms are more inclusive and heterogeneous.

In this new society, people will be changing jobs approximately every five years. The demands of these new jobs will require skills associated with team membership; listening; self-management; time management; assuming responsibility; and following schedules (Secretary's Commission on Achieving Necessary Skills, 1991).

There is a strong relationship between the needs of the workforce and classroom management (Goleman, 1998). Goleman's research found that *lack of self-control* is a primary factor for lack of success in the workforce, with a sense of helplessness and frequent distractions as the most important reasons for poor job performance. In contrast, high job performance occurs when there are high expectations of employees who are allowed to set their own goals for achieving these expectations, when the employees receive prompt feedback, and exhibit good listening skills (Cummings, 2000).

States are currently attempting to revamp education to meet the demands of the twenty-first century by including life skills, a wide range of intellectual skills, and social skills. There is agreement between leaders in both industry and academia that students have to learn to become innovative, solve problems, and interact successfully with people from many different cultures (Gewertz, 2008).

While some are concerned that our students will be able to compete in a global economy and believe that our economy is a function of how effective schools are at preparing future workers, others disagree. "For individual students, school achievement is only weakly related to subsequent workplace performance. And for nations, there's little correlation between average test scores and economic vigor" (Kohn, 2007, p. 1).

Parenting styles have changed within the past thirty years from a tendency to be more rigid and authoritarian with a do-as-I-say-because-I-said-so approach to a more nurturing permissive do-as-you-want approach to bringing up children. Research has indicated, however, that neither of these approaches used by parents, or teachers for that matter, will prepare children for the twenty-first century (Steinberg, 1996; Marzano, 2003a).

What is most effective is an *authoritative* (not authoritarian) approach that "balances nurturing with setting clear limits, giving guidance without controlling, seeks input from children for important decisions, sets high standards of responsibility, and encourages independence, not dependency" (Cummings, 2000, p. 9).

## Adapting Classrooms to Societal Changes

Though this is not a book on effective instruction per se, it is a given that dynamic curriculum and instruction are integral to and major partners in effective classroom management. Before you can consider curriculum, you must be aware of your students' price point. A price point is the amount of money a consumer is willing to expend on travel, clothing, household items, and so on. It would be useless for a salesperson to attempt to sell goods or services for which the purchaser will not pay.

For your students to "consume" the curriculum, you must know that their price point is the content they are ready to learn *before* you can plan curriculum. Content that is too easy or familiar and that which is too advanced will lead to confusion and discontent that could lead to classroom management problems (Peterson, 2010). To determine the students' price point, you must make the effort to learn enough about them before school begins.

Curriculum and instruction also have to reflect the needs of the twenty-first century. This means that students must be involved meaningfully in learning, because if they are not, they will find their own ways to become engaged, often to the detriment of themselves and to the rest of the class.

Students should be invited to add their own curriculum goals in addition to those of the teacher; be given choices regarding how they will learn; self-reflect and monitor their goal achievement; redirect their effort, when necessary; and play an essential role in their own assessment/evaluation. It is noteworthy that attention to the development of student independence has been lacking in teacher education programs (Kaufman & Moss, 2010).

Students should be involved in relevant experiences and authentic problems, and when age appropriate, should participate in constructing scoring rubrics. Depending on the situation, students may work independently or in groups, check each other's work, and coach when warranted, with all individual members taking responsibility for the group's achievements and supporting each other to attain success.

When implementing an effective curriculum, the teacher relies less on lectures and sequential lessons than on active, project-based, hands-on learning. In this environment students learn skills and concepts entrenched in these activities, which are accompanied by fluid time frames. The teacher uses primary sources, inside as well as outside resources, and electronics as opposed to the textbook or worksheets as predominant means of instruction.

Wolk (2008) suggests that we introduce "joy" in learning. Some ways this may be accomplished is by providing students choices; allowing students to create things; reading good books; having some fun together; showing off students' work; and providing them time to tinker.

All the above critical curriculum and instructional attributes have classroom management implications. Ensuring that these attributes are implemented will go far in eliminating many improper student behaviors.

To accommodate for the requirements of students in twenty-first century classrooms, organizational structures such as modular (block) scheduling with longer time assigned to some classes, multiage grouping, and looping (keeping the same teacher with the same students over several years) have been implemented. These changes have made managing the classroom more multifaceted and complex.

As classrooms in the twenty-first century become more student-centered, both teachers and students must adjust accordingly. Classrooms are now becoming learning communities in which there is *shared responsibility* for the success of all community members. Within this context there has been a shift in emphasis from teacher control to the student's taking more responsibility not only for his or her own learning but also for managing the classroom.

While in the past teachers were taught to control student behavior, now teachers are focusing on developing strategies that support students' making good choices (McLeod et al., 2003). Teachers and students listen carefully to each other. Feedback is prompt on the part of both. There is a sharing of leadership between teachers and students as the teacher no longer controls but fosters student self-control and responsibility.

**TABLE 1.1**
Changes in Approaches to Classroom Management

| Past View | Twenty-first-century View |
| --- | --- |
| Atmosphere of Competition | Atmosphere of Cooperation |
| Teacher Control | Student Self-Control |
| Teacher Leadership | Shared Leadership |
| Teacher as Sole Instructor | Teacher as Coach and Facilitator |
| Conformity | Innovation |

The teacher's role is one of a guide and coach as opposed to pouring information and rules into students' heads. The teacher determines rules collaboratively with students and there is shared responsibility for implementing and enforcing rules. This sharing is particularly important because "a sense of efficacy, control, or self-determination is critical if people are to feel intrinsically motivated. When people come to believe that the events and outcomes in their lives are mostly uncontrollable, they have developed learned helplessness" (Woolfolk, 2008, p. 371).

The classroom atmosphere is warm, friendly, and caring. All class members have mutual respect for and support each other in a spirit of cooperation in which all have a stake in the success of all other members. It is the purpose of this book to assist you in using these principles to improve your skills toward being a shared leader in classroom management.

As with any school plan, contemporary classroom management will be a challenge for you to implement unless you have the support of all parties in your school and district. In many cases, we are not there yet.

## Theoretical Underpinnings That Support Twenty-First-Century Views of Classroom Management

The same theories that guide learning also apply to classroom management, especially in view of the needs of the twenty-first-century classroom. These theories include behavioral, cognitive, and constructivist approaches.

Behaviorism. When considering behaviorism, traditional associations that come to mind are often token economies, contingency contracting, and group consequences. Though these remain at the core of behavior theory, more recently, self-management/self-regulation has been an emphasis and application of the behavioral perspective. Moreover, the need for students to be responsible for and involved in self-regulating is so pervasive in the research that *all* theories support this need (Mace et al., 2001).

Effective self-management depends on setting one's own goals (Pintrich & Schunk, 2002) and publicizing them (Hayes et al., 1985). In addition, monitoring and assessing goals are critical behaviors in self-regulation, especially when students have established criteria upon which to base their assessment. Students are then able to modify and improve their behavior and compare their performance with prior behavior (Mace et al., 2001).

Cognitive. While behaviorists see students' learning and behavior as a result of external stimuli, the cognitive view sees learning and behavior as internal mental processes. Students are actively involved in the way they process information (Ashcraft, 2002). Knowledge, memory, thinking, and problem solving are areas for development. Spurred by the work of Piaget (1954), knowledge is viewed as symbolic mental constructs, or schemata. When the student' schemata are changed, learning takes place. As students acquire knowledge, this knowledge itself facilitates a change in behavior.

Constructivism. The theoretical basis for constructivism also comes largely from the work of Piaget (1963, 1964). The core idea in constructivism is that knowledge is *constructed* as students build new knowledge on the basis of what they have already learned. The student is *not* a passive receiver of transmitted information. Therefore, as students enter learning situations with knowledge acquired from previous experiences, their prior knowledge influences what new or modified knowledge they will build from the new learning experiences.

To build from the new experiences, learning must be active. If the new experience is inconsistent with students' present knowledge, this knowledge must be adjusted to accommodate the new experience. The constructivist teacher is curious about students' current understanding, provides experiences in which students are actively involved, allows student responses to guide subsequent lessons, promotes relevant experiential learning, and fosters self-reflection.

While the constructivist theory described above concentrates on how students make meaning on their own, *social* constructivists believe that students construct knowledge by interacting with each other. The social context is emphasized in learning where social interaction involving cultural history, customs, and language activities determines individual learning (Vygotsky, 1997). Since the culture provides the cognitive tools needed for development, involved parents and teachers as well as older students are given a greater role in this development.

The implications of learning theory to classroom management are clear. Student self-regulation with student ownership of classroom management should be encouraged. Student-centric approaches such as active participation, relevant experiences, and self-reflection should be applied. With teacher guidance, students should be actively involved in all phases of classroom management.

The common threads of student input, student autonomy, control and involvement; shared responsibility; and sense of community should be incorporated into all aspects of contemporary classroom management. At this point it would be critical to remind you that even though your ultimate goal is having students manage their own behavior, you are ultimately responsible for the behavior of *all* students in your classroom (Canter, 2006).

After you review and master general guidelines in part 1 to help you improve managing the contemporary classroom successfully, you will increase your repertoire by learning specific strategies (systems, models) for handling student behavior problems, especially those which are more challenging, in part 2.

## Classroom Management and Student Misbehavior

When thinking of classroom management, problems with student misbehavior frequently come first to mind. Misbehavior problems are often associated with discipline or punishment, though discipline and punishment are *distinctly different*. Discipline is guiding the student's personal, social, and cognitive development in a way that will minimize misbehavior thus making punishment, the imposition of a penalty, unnecessary.

Make no mistake about it. *All teachers have classroom behavior problems.* It is the main complaint about their job (Kottler et al., 2005). Some teachers have fewer discipline problems than others, and if you implement the guidelines presented in this book, your problems should be minimal.

There are several kinds of student misbehaviors ranging from minor to serious.

Class disruptions. It has been reported consistently that 95 percent of all classroom behavior problems consistently fall into the category of class disruptions (Jones 1979, 1987, 2000). Of these, 80 percent are *talking problems* such as chatting with a friend, speaking out of turn, whispering, speaking loudly, or calling out. The remaining 15 percent are *movement problems* such as passing notes, tossing or shooting objects (paper airplanes, rubber bands, spitballs), fooling around, gesturing, and getting out of the seat to go to the pencil sharpener or the lavatory without permission.

It has been confirmed that 5 percent of students consistently cause the major problems (Curwin & Mendler, 1999, Curwin et al, 2008). The good news is that if teachers can keep the talking and movement problems under control, they will be 95 percent on the way to having effective classroom behavior.

The other 5 percent of problems in order of least to most severe include:

- Goofing off. Students may be off task, daydreaming, doodling, sleeping, or doing work not related to the lesson.

- Defying authority. A student refuses to do what the teacher wants, and may even become hostile in not cooperating with any school activity.
- Moral issues. A student may be involved in stealing, cheating, lying, or improper sexual activity.
- Aggression/violence. A student may physically or verbally attack a teacher or another student. Carrying lethal weapons to school and dealing in or taking drugs are serious misbehaviors that could disrupt the entire school. Many of these students are subjected to severe problems. These include: homelessness, depression, tendency toward suicide, eating disorders, alcoholic parents, attention deficit and hyperactivity disorder, incarcerated parents, poverty, and sexual and physical abuse, and the statistics associated with these problem areas are shocking (Marzano, 2003b).
- Students who are bullies demonstrate oppositional defiant disorders (ODD) and who have anger management issues also fall into this category (Boynton & Boynton, 2005). Moreover, gang membership is increasing nationally and particularly in the previously immune suburbs. "What lures youths to gangs is prevalent everywhere: peer pressure, boredom, the desire for money, the need to belong and parental neglect" (Worley, 2006, p. 10A).

Research has indicated that new teachers especially may lack the training to handle more severe behaviors and their causes as described above (Smart & Igo, 2010). Even if you have experience, you may not be able to handle aggressive and violent behaviors that come up in your classroom by yourself. To deal with these situations you should consult immediately with the trained specialists in your school/district to give you support.

As a shared leader with your students in classroom management, however, it is in your interest to believe that you have the capability of influencing all students to behave positively, *including those who are chronically disruptive*. Some excuses frequently given for these students include conditions listed previously: coming from a dysfunctional family, having a low socioeconomic status; living in a high-crime neighborhood; being classified as having special needs; or having emotional problems. Canter (2006) challenges these excuses, indicating that these students *can* control their behavior.

As evidence, Cantor cites the fact that these students behave when the principal or special outside visitor is in the room, when they have to take a standardized test, when given a reward, or on the days the teachers does not feel good and is, therefore, less likely to tolerate misbehavior. Also, these students often behave properly the first few days of school and with other teachers. So it is not a question of whether they *can* behave as much as it is whether they *will* they behave.

Canter (2006) also states that the *only* exception in which a student cannot control behavior occurs when it involves an organic disorder such as schizophrenia or autism or when a student is subject to seizures.

It is useful to point out that "Misbehavior is to a classroom what pain is to a body—a useful status report that something isn't working as it should" (Sylwester, 2000, p. 23). The misbehavior is *symptomatic* of an underlying problem. In addressing this problem, the teacher may have to not only examine the needs of a particular student but also address the way she or he and all class members interact with that student and with each other.

As you read through the following guidelines in this text, reflect on your current classroom management practices and how consistent they are with the demands of the twenty-first century.

# 2

# Proactive Approaches to Classroom Management

BEFORE CONTINUING WITH A DISCUSSION of proactive approaches to classroom management, it is valuable to remind you of the attributes of the twenty-first-century classroom. As you continue to read not only this chapter but the remainder of this book, try to anticipate how these twenty-first-century contemporary approaches can be applied.

### Attributes of Twenty-First-Century Classroom Management
- Student-centered
- Shared control by all class members
- Student participation in making, implementing, and enforcing rules
- Constant feedback from teacher to students, from students to teacher, and from students to students
- Increase in student responsibility
- Teacher helps student make good choices
- Teacher fosters student self-control
- Careful listening among all class members including the teacher
- Classroom atmosphere warm, friendly, and caring
- All class members have mutual respect for and support each other in a spirit of cooperation
- All have a stake in the success of all other members
- All class members are bonded with each other

## Extending Kounin's Preventive Research to Contemporary Classrooms

Just as in medicine it is better for the patient and more cost-effective to prevent disease, so is classroom problem prevention better for both you and your students. It has been reported that 90 percent of classroom management occurs *before* students misbehave (Franklin, 2006).

In a study that has become an educational classic, Kounin (1970) compared problem-free classrooms with those that were disruptive. He found that teachers in both types of classrooms usually handled disruptive problems similarly *once they arose*, but the teachers who had few problems were those who used certain preventive techniques. Kounin identified these as *withitness, group focus, overlapping,* and *movement management.*

### Withitness

It is likely that you were at one time a student in a classroom where a teacher seemed to be in his own world, oblivious to what was actually going on. Groups of students may have been talking, some reading material not relevant to class, others doing homework for another class. Twenty-first-century classroom managers want to ensure that all students are involved.

Teachers who have withitness are aware of everything going on in the classroom whether they are looking directly at the students or not. These teachers' antennae are pointed in all directions. They interact with everyone, not with just a few who are allowed to monopolize attention. Eye contact is maintained with all students, making them realize that the teacher is noticing their behavior. A withit teacher knows who the real troublemakers are, intervenes quickly before disruption gets out of control, and when two or more problems are brewing, handles the more (most) serious one first.

Whereas the traditional teacher might be satisfied being just withit, a contemporary classroom manager goes beyond. He or she seeks feedback from students to determine *why* they may not be meaningfully engaged. This teacher constantly asks him- or herself why some students may be on the brink of or be actually involved in misbehavior, analyzes the problem with the class, and proceeds to correct the problem with class recommendations, whenever appropriate.

### Group Focus

A teacher who demonstrates group focus keeps all students involved during instruction. If one student is misbehaving, the teacher communicates expectations through the "ripple effect," correcting that misbehavior to alert students in the rest of the group considering or exhibiting the same misbehavior to correct theirs.

The teacher moves about the room to check the work of different groups, employing current techniques to keep everyone on target. Students may temporarily conduct or continue with a lesson. A group of students may write answers to questions and check each other's answers. The teacher constantly circulates about the room to keep in physical contact with everyone.

Kounin's emphasis on the importance of having the teacher moving around the room has been supported by the research of Hall (1977), Scollon (1985), and Bowers & Flinders (1991). Student involvement varies directly with distance from the teacher. The closer the distance between teacher and student, the greater is student involvement and communication, with less opportunity for the student to become disruptive.

Here again, the contemporary classroom manager, while involved with group focus, wants to know *why* the students may be misbehaving. This teacher asks the students for their input and assesses the situation accordingly. As shared leaders in classroom management, students are responsible for implementing and enforcing classroom rules. The *students* alert misbehaving students regarding their responsibilities to themselves and to the rest of the class.

### Overlapping

The teacher with overlapping skills keeps on top of several different activities at the same time. She may check one student's math, spelling, or lab report while keeping an eye on a small group, or work with one group that is writing a play while supervising two other groups who have different assignments regarding that play. If a student from a group other than one the teacher is working with raises a hand, the teacher uses a gesture to acknowledge the student *without interrupting* the group with whom the teacher is working.

In twenty-first-century classrooms, the teacher-coach makes sure that students within each group have assigned responsibilities, not only to each member of the group but to all other class members as well. Students have input regarding what these responsibilities should be and how to implement them. They are agreed to collaboratively, clarified, and practiced so that all students know what to do regarding their assignment, how each member will contribute to that assignment, and how to handle any problems that may occur.

### Movement Management

The teacher who can manage movement keeps the class active at an appropriate pace. He has a sense of timing, knowing when to speed up, or change the activity. There is an absence of slowdowns where the lesson comes to a standstill, or when students do not have anything to do when they have finished their work.

Slowdowns also occur through *overdwelling*, commonly referred to as "beating a dead horse," where the teacher keeps teaching content (or rules) long after the students have mastered them. Transitions (see chapter 4) from one activity to another are smooth, and there is an avoidance of *flip-flops*, where the teacher begins an activity, then reverts back to the prior one; *dangles*, where the teacher begins an activity, then stops and leaves it hanging; or *fragmentation*, where the teacher breaks up a learning activity into *very* small segments.

It is interesting to note that even though Kounin's work was introduced in the 1970s, his suggestions are still supported (Emmer et al., 2003a; 2003b).

The contemporary classroom manager can avoid many of the ineffective behaviors indicated above by relying less on whole group instruction and focusing more on group work, especially after an initial lesson has been introduced. In the spirit of involving students in classroom management, the contemporary teacher asks the students for their suggestions regarding what activities might be offered when completing work ahead of time, what signals they might give the teacher when they feel that they "got it" so that overdwelling is not necessary, and when and how instruction can be changed to be more effective, thereby avoiding flip-flops, dangles, and fragmentation.

When extending Kounin's preventive techniques to contemporary classroom management, the teacher as coach and the students should remind misbehaving students when their behavior is not supporting other class members and interferes with the learning of others. As such, this misbehavior will not foster the cooperation that will lead to the success of every student in the class, which is an integral attribute for the twenty-first-century classroom.

### Self-Reflection

How aware are you regarding what is going on with *all* students, whether you are looking at them or not? Give recent examples.

How meaningfully involved are all your students both during instruction and after they have completed their work?

How do you usually handle lack of attention/student involvement?

What evidence can you give that you are able to manage several different activities simultaneously?

What do you do to keep the momentum of your class flowing without interruption?

How involved are your students in making classroom management decisions? How have you used your students to correct the misbehavior of other students?

## Creating a Positive Classroom Atmosphere

Besides the preventive measures described by Kounin (1970), there are other proactive techniques teachers can use to establish a successful learning community. The most important of these is creating positive student-teacher and student-student relationships in a classroom where all feel welcome and are responsible for making other class members welcome.

The contemporary classroom manager might say something like this to the class: "We are in this together. When one of us succeeds, we all succeed. When one of us fails, we all fail. It is critically important to me personally that all of us do well." This is a very powerful message. Of course, *the teacher must implement the implications of this message consistently.*

To emphasize the above, Brooks (2011) has described the successful classroom as engaging and well-managed. In this classroom there is a strong interrelationship between student and teacher in an atmosphere of trust in which students feel free to participate. Brooks promotes the idea that there is a partnership between classroom management and student learning. Both thrive when trusting, respectful, caring relationships exist between students and teachers. Only then will rules become effective and students become engaged learners.

In constructing this positive classroom climate, three main factors should be considered. They involve the students, the teacher, and the learning environment itself.

### The Students

It has been a criticism of teachers and administrators that they do not ask the right questions when it comes to classroom management (Kohn, 2003). Kohn suggests that instead of asking how we can get students to obey, we should ask what our students need and how we, as educators, can meet those needs. Because we are focused on getting students to conform, we fall back on practices of doing things *to* them as opposed to working *with* them. This section will concentrate on working with students.

Fundamental to contemporary classroom management is fostering caring relationships and finding positive characteristics of students Rigsbee (2008). There are many different ways to accomplish these.

Kohn (1996) makes the point that students do not become more likely to think for themselves or care about others when teachers take all the responsibility for rules and expectations for student behavior and consequences for noncompliance. He encourages teachers to assist students in becoming compassionate, in assuming responsibility, and to take the unpredictable and likely messy route that involves having the students work together in deciding how to be fair and in determining what respect means.

Traditional approaches to classroom management would likely have teachers informing students what rules would be expected to be followed. Twenty-first-century managers, however, show students that they are respected, valued, and trusted by giving them a stake in the successful operation of the classroom.

Successful contemporary managers *have students participate in establishing rules and procedures* (Curwin & Mendler, 1999; Marzano, 2003b, 2007), *and do so at the very beginning of school.* A rule conveys a general expectation that can be applied in many different circumstances, such as "Listen when others are speaking"; a procedure states a course of action for a routine, such as a method for passing out or collecting materials. Rules/procedures should be reasonable, clear, short, *explained*, practiced when applicable, displayed, and minimal with approximately five to eight for elementary school students (Emmer et al., 2003a) and around seven for middle/secondary (Emmer et al., 2003b).

There is a difference between behavior and classroom management. Behavior is related to discipline and classroom management has to do with procedures and routines. According to Wong and Wong (2005), teachers who are ineffective discipline students with consequences and punishments, whereas teachers who are effective manage their classrooms with procedures, rules, and routines.

Taking time to explain rules and procedures is highly recommended because in order to be implemented, they must be understood (Good & Brophy, 2003). It is also effective to explain the reasons *why* the rules are important. This practice is especially important for students whose cultures may not be compatible with rules and procedures normally implemented in American classrooms.

Rules should be *reasonable*. There are four criteria for reasonable rules and procedures. They must be necessary, capable of being performed by the students, not run against human nature, and not require for their enforcement more resources than you can afford (McLeod et al., 2003). When establishing rules, the teacher should concentrate not only on what to do with students who do not comply with the rules, but more importantly on what these students are being asked to do (Kohn, 1996).

Effective classroom managers are aware of the importance of making instruction more personal by getting to know their students by name right away and immediately *calling them by name.* Contemporary classroom managers make it a point to learn something personal about each student and *use* this information in instruction. When students are involved personally, they become more involved emotionally. And "emotions . . . are not the cards at the game table but the table itself" (Jensen, 2005, p. 80).

How often have you been in two or three classes with the same instructor who still did not know your name? How connected and involved did that make you feel?

Learning students' names and positive information about them quickly may be more difficult in departmentalized classes, prevalent in middle/high schools where teachers can be assigned 125 students or more. Still, make a concerted effort to know each student, *and the sooner the better.* Plan an activity to have all your students get to know each other by name, also, and address each other by name during class.

Some teachers distribute five-by-eight index cards to all age-appropriate students and ask them to write a symbol or word that best describes them. Then, each student in turn states his or her name, what the rest of the students should know about him or her, and explains what the symbol or word communicates.

Whenever the occasion allows, offer students the opportunity to talk about themselves. "People like to talk about themselves and the things that interest them" (Marzano, 2007, p. 114). Providing this activity allows students to remain emotionally involved in learning, especially when you connect what you know about them personally and/or their interests to the knowledge and skills to be studied.

As a contemporary manager who is aware of feedback provided by students, show that you are aware of and sensitive to students' feelings. Try to pick up on attitudes that may come across in art work, written work, or during discussions. *You teach students how to treat you and each other by the way you treat them.* If you show respect for and are courteous and sensitive to all students, they will tend to model your behavior back toward you and toward each other.

In the culturally diverse twenty-first-century classroom, be genuinely curious about different cultures represented by your students. However, always remember that each individual is different and may not conform to the cultural norm. Social scientists will confirm that there are greater differences between individuals *within* a group than there are *between* groups. This fact is so important that you should repeat it to yourself. Ask students to share their customs with you and capitalize on these customs during instruction. Also, try to demonstrate that you have *heard* and understand students' feelings by paraphrasing some of their comments made in frustration or anger.

Paraphrasing by teachers was promoted by Gordon (1974) and is still effective today. If a student says, "I hate chemistry," you, as a sensitive, supportive teacher, could paraphrase by saying, "You're having difficulty balancing this equation" (paraphrase). Then you could add, "Let's see if we can work together to balance it."

Make sure that all students are active participants in *meaningful* activities. Prepare a sociogram for each class. Identify who are the *isolates*, the students selected by no one or very few classmates as those with whom they would like to work, and the *stars*, the students picked by many classmates as those with whom they would like to work.

Attempt to pair or group the isolates into instructional activities with more socially accepted students so that all will feel welcome in the class. Isolates will be more welcomed by socially accepted students if you have at the beginning of school established and then continuously reinforced a supportive classroom environment.

In recent school shootings, one common factor regarding the perpetrators was that they were loners. Some reasons for feeling that they were loners could be explained by a popular song that conveys the message that you are only somebody when somebody loves you and cares about you. In a successful learning community everyone should feel as though he or she is *somebody* and that all class members, especially the teacher, are bonded with and care about him or her. Bonding is especially critical for middle and high school students.

> Being liked by teachers can offset the effects of peer rejection in middle school. And, students who have few friends, but are not rejected—simply ignored by other students—can remain well-adjusted academically and socially when they are liked and supported by teachers (Woolfolk, 2008, p. 453).

Formerly, there was an emphasis on what students could *not* do. As a twenty-first-century classroom manager, go out of your way to identify the strengths of each student. Let students use their strengths and interests in helping you set goals, modes of instruction, and assessment. When a student accomplishes a task, be sure to encourage him or her.

A productive way to encourage is by sending "You" messages. Consider the difference between the two columns in table 2.1.

**TABLE 2.1**
**Comparing "You" and "I" Messages**

| "You" Messages | "I" Messages (General) |
| --- | --- |
| You did a great job helping Larry learn his multiplication facts. | I think you did a great job helping Larry with multiplication. |
| You worked so hard on your composition that you raised your score 10 points. | I'm proud that you raised your score 10 points. |
| You cleaned up so well after lab that the other students imitated you. | I liked the way you cleaned up your lab table. |

In the past teachers were advised to use "I" messages, statements regarding what the teacher thinks or feels. The control was in the hands of the teacher. In a student-centric classroom "You" messages emphasize the positives that *students* have performed, not what you feel about what they've done. In the "You" messages the student is in control. (Note other versions of "I" messages described in chapter 3.) Students should feel positive about what *they* have achieved and what control they have taken in applying their own effort.

## Summary: Establishing a Positive Learning Environment Involving Students

- Have students help in establishing rules and procedures.
- Have students help in deciding positive consequences for following rules and procedures and negative consequences for not following them.
- Learn students' names and something personal about them right away.
- Use students' interests in lessons.
- Be sensitive to students' feelings.
- Engage students in meaningful activities.
- Identify and build on strengths of each student.

### Self-Reflection

How have you involved your students in establishing rules and procedures?
How long does it usually take you to learn your students' names? Do you then immediately call them by name?
What do you know about your students personally?
What have you done to show that you are sensitive to students' feelings?
What meaningful activities do you provide for your students?
How have you tried to include all students in these activities? How successful were you?
How have you made all students feel welcome?
How have you capitalized on student strengths?

## The Teacher

Positive teacher behavior is an effective problem preventer. There are several positive teacher behaviors worth noting.

If there was ever an occupation requiring a sense of humor, it is teaching. If you have one, you possess many advantages. Interacting positively with students is easier, teaching is less stressful, and students enjoy your classes more. In addition to having a sense of humor, you should also be willing to laugh, *even at yourself,* when unanticipated humorous events occur in the classroom.

As a shared leader, never lose sight of the fact that you are a role model, a *critical* role model for your students. Behave as a mature person they can look up to by using proper speech, grammar, and by dressing professionally. While clothes may not make a person, they can be major factors in *un*making a person (Wong & Wong, 1998).

> Research reveals that the clothing worn by teachers affects the work, attitude, and discipline of students. You dress for four main effects:
> 1. Respect
> 2. Credibility
> 3. Acceptance
> 4. Authority (Wong & Wong, 1998, p. 55).

Teachers often complain that they do not get the respect awarded other professions. Their colleagues retort that those teachers may not be well groomed, may even speak and behave like the students, making it difficult for *all* teachers to gain public and student respect.

Some dos and don'ts are listed in table 2.2 when using language in the classroom were recommended by Ryan et al. (2008).

Shared learning partners admit to making a mistake or not knowing an answer to a question. This behavior on your part shows that you are a person who takes responsibility, thus providing a good example for your students. They will also respect you more for your admission. Convey the message that it is all right to make mistakes. We all do, and what is most significant about mistakes is that we learn from them and try to do better; mistakes help us grow. And if we do not know the answer to a question, what is even more important is that we learn how to find the answer.

Establish a positive but realistic level of expectation not only for academics but also for behavior. When working with the students to establish rules and procedures, convey the attitude that you know your students can learn subject matter and behave properly, and *do not give up on any student*. The confidence you exhibit will often give students the extra incentive they may need.

**TABLE 2.2**
**Professional Classroom Speech**

| Dos | Don'ts |
| --- | --- |
| Speak clearly and concisely | Use filler words such as "uh," "like," "you know" |
| Use gender-neutral terms or address students as "class" or "boys and girls." | Address students as "guys," "you guys," or "fellows" |
| Use proper grammar | Use expletives or profanity |

(Adapted from Ryan et al., 2008, p. 75)

Many successful people can trace their success, or possibly their redirection in life, to the fact that one person, usually a teacher, believed in them and encouraged them, especially with the support of the class. *You* have the potential to be that person.

As an example, Scott Brown from Massachusetts, who was elected to replace the late Ted Kennedy in the U.S. Senate, was on the MSNBC show, *Morning Joe*, on February 21, 2011, to promote his book, *Against All Odds*. In this book Senator Brown describes his early life where he was surrounded by a family in which there was alcoholism and physical abuse. Given this environment it would seem that Brown would have had a lot of difficulty adjusting and "making it."

However, he then related an event which was not in the book. The incident occurred when a middle-school teacher dragged Scott into a private room, looked him straight in the eye and said, "You could become somebody." This was a very powerful message the teacher delivered because at the time, Brown was fighting "against all odds." He indicated that this statement by the teacher actually turned his life around as evidenced by the fact that he became a lawyer and a U.S. senator.

As a contemporary classroom manager, be responsive to students' reactions and feedback by constantly assessing and changing immediately, with the suggestions of the students, whatever instruction or method of dealing with improper behavior is not working. Model flexibility by trying out new teaching strategies, new materials, or new activities. If you are not particularly creative or innovative, you can still be resourceful.

At this point it would be useful to note that it is a myth for teachers to think that all misbehavior problems can be prevented, even if dynamic materials and activities are used to keep students' interest (Long & Frye, 1985). Some students are subject to mood swings and peer and home problems, which could affect the classroom even when the teacher offers exciting experiences.

In a successful learning community, a teacher wants to promote a cooperative spirit through shared leadership and developing student self-control. Show that you are aware of the fact that "control over one's life is something that everyone wants and needs. When we don't get it, we go after control over others. Because many of our discipline problems in school either start or end with a power struggle, it is a good idea to look at the idea of sharing control with the students" (McLeod et al., 2003, p. 66).

One small caveat regarding self-control should be pointed out. In some cases self-control could be inhibitory, especially in the situation when the self-control does not make sense. When exercising self-control, it is more important to have the ability to choose whether and/or when to control oneself rather than merely comply in every situation (Kohn, 2008).

An example would be exhibiting self-control in not pushing another student. However, if an object was about to fall upon that student, it would be beneficial to push him or her out of the way.

Offer students structured choices. Doing so communicates to students that they are competent, in control within limits, and responsible for their own behavior (Fay & Funk, 1995). Besides, choice helps students practice decision making, allows opportunities for students to showcase themselves, and helps students learn that school is relevant to their lives. For teachers, choice is the best way to differentiate (Tedrow, 2008).

Choices can be offered for behavior as well as for instruction. The choices should be authentic and mutually acceptable. There is no point in asking a student if she prefers to miss gym or complete an assignment if going to gym is her favorite activity.

Interact with your students in a friendly (not overfriendly) but businesslike manner. "A businesslike classroom refers to a learning environment in which the students and the teacher conduct themselves in ways suggesting that achieving specified learning goals takes priority over other concerns" (Cangelosi, 2008, p. 58). Remember that you do not have to be loved by your students; you have to be respected.

"Students do not like or respect teachers who let them get away with misbehavior. The foundation of student respect is based on the premise that you and the class care enough about each other to make sure they behave in a manner that is in their best interest and the best interest of others" (Canter, 2006, p. 26). But you should also note that students like teachers who are trusting and caring and who treat students with respect. When students believe that teachers care for and value them, the students are more cooperative in complying with teachers' requests. These teachers have more influence on students than teachers not so perceived (Jones & Jones, 2003).

Caring teachers→→→Student appreciation→→→Student cooperation

Be fair but firm. Keep your promises and avoid reprimanding or punishing the entire class when only a few are responsible for misbehavior. When some students are misbehaving, have the class first discuss the misbehavior and then determine what should be done about it before you intervene.

Part of being fair is being aware of the halo effect: "the tendency to view particular aspects of students based on a general impression, either positive or negative" (Woolfolk, 2008, p. 618). For example, when a student is particularly cooperative or friendly, a teacher may assign a higher grade based on those attributes instead of on what the student actually achieved, or assuming that a student who is a member of a particular ethnic group will be a behavior problem.

Do not necessarily accept other teachers' evaluations of students. Students behave differently with different teachers, and it may be what the teacher does that causes students to behave in certain (undesirable or desirable) ways. It is also essential to remember that in today's diverse classroom settings, fair no longer means treating everyone the same but "trying to make sure each student gets what she needs in order to grow and succeed" (Tomlinson, 2001, p. 23).

### Summary: Establishing a Positive Classroom Atmosphere with Respect to the Teacher

- Display a sense of humor.
- Remember that you are a critical role model.
- Admit mistakes.
- Establish a positive level of expectation.
- Be responsive to students' reactions.
- Share leadership and control.
- Present students with choices.
- Relate to students in a friendly yet businesslike manner.
- Be firm but fair.

### Self-Reflection

How is your sense of humor?
What choices do you offer students?
What kind of role model are you?
What have you done recently that demonstrates that you are flexible?
How firm are you with your students?
How do you demonstrate fairness with your students?
What situation could occur in your classroom where student self-control would not make sense?

## The Learning Environment

Contemporary classroom managers ensure that they establish a positive classroom learning environment. There are several ways to establish this type of environment.

*Provide physical and emotional safety.* Ensure that all students feel safe, both physically and emotionally (Jensen, 1998). The classroom must be a place where students feel they can take risks, ask questions, answer questions, make mistakes, admit they do not know an answer, or come up with a "wacky" idea without verbal or nonverbal ridicule from anyone in the class (Tomlinson, 2001).

*Show enthusiasm.* Create a learning environment in which your enthusiasm is picked up by the students. It is likely that you have been in classrooms where the teacher did not seem to want to be there, and/or even appeared bored, which made it more difficult for you to feel excited. Make every student feel important by arranging some work the student can display or present.

Videotape students working on meaningful projects or students not working productively. Show the video and have the students provide input regarding how *their* work habits were successful, or how productivity/behavior can be improved. Take pictures of students who are meaningfully and actively involved and display their pictures on the bulletin board with an appropriate title such as, "We Are Great," or "We're Almost There." Hard work gives students a feeling of accomplishment.

*Always have enough for the students to do.* Free or unstructured time is conducive to off-task behavior. Typically, these times occur when students enter the room, when the teacher takes the roll, or when students finish their work ahead of time.

Sponge activities are *substantive* learning activities that absorb free time and can be recommended by or negotiated with students. Sponge activities may include: reading a book, working on a computer program, completing a project at the learning activity center, or completing a warm-up assignment that is written on the board so that students have something to work on when they enter the classroom (Boynton & Boynton, 2005).

*Provide opportunities for all to succeed.* Set up an environment in which you teach for success and there is a pervasive expectation of progress. Evaluate work and assignments to ensure that students are not involved in busy work but are being challenged at their cognitive levels.

When appropriate, give students choices of goals, methods of implementation, and methods of assessment. Use scoring rubrics as teaching tools to assist students in self-improving. When age appropriate, involve students in constructing scoring rubrics. Provide the appropriate amount of stress. Not enough stress offers students little or no challenge, and too much stress turns them off (Jensen, 1998).

*Give students a break occasionally.* It boosts morale to skip an assignment or a quiz, or to do something of one's choice for a period instead of the designated activity for that period. Get students' input with respect to breaks they might enjoy.

*Connect and interconnect.* Make a sincere attempt to bond with all students and ensure that all students feel bonded with each other. Show that you are interested in your students as people.

Try to have a personal "chat" with each student to find out more about them all and what together you can do to make each one successful. "When teachers consciously had personal conversations with students for more than two minutes at a time over 10 days . . . they saw an 85% improvement in classroom management for that student" (Franklin, 2006, p. 5). Franklin uses the analogy of a cramped muscle in dealing with students, especially the most behavior-challenged. Students desire a positive personal connection with an adult authority figure, and when they get that positive connection, the muscle relaxes over time, leaving the students free to concentrate on learning (Franklin, 2006).

*Acknowledge the personal/positive.* Occasionally *recognize* something personal or positive in each student. Statements such as, "You wear a lot of bright shirts," or, "You've shown great improvement in your computation skills," go a long way in keeping you and your students connected. When a student behaves in a positive manner or accomplishes a challenging task for his or her performance level, it would be worth your while to recognize these achievements by communicating with the home through calling, sending an e-mail, a note, or a certificate of good behavior/accomplishment (Marzano, 2007).

*Create a learning environment that is safe from bullies.* Bullying in schools has become a scourge in this country. Researchers have seen in one study that students who bullied other students rarely did this alone and that bystanders were involved in 85 percent of bullying incidents (Viadero, 2010). It has been reported that "bullies, their victims, bystanders, parents, teachers, and other adults in the building are all part of an ecology in schools that can either sustain or suppress bullying behaviors" (Viadero, 2010, p. 1)

Fifteen percent of the school population has suffered extreme anxieties from bullies with 75 to 90 percent having experienced some kind of harassment (Hoover & Oliver, 1996). In a study conducted at the University of Florida (2008), it was reported that in particular, social bullying in adolescence such as gossiping or spreading rumors has been linked with anxiety and depression in the victims during early adulthood.

It is also important for you be alert to potential bullies. Contrary to the perception that bullies are the most popular students or most socially outcast, research conducted over a several-year period found that students in the middle of the school social hierarchies are more likely to be bullies (Shah, 2011a). Early detection is particularly critical because several studies have indicated that bullying on the part of young children may be early signs of violent tendencies, delinquency, and criminality (Orloff, 2008).

Even though they have problems in and out of school, bullies are not always disliked. Many achieve high social status (Rodkin et al., 2000). Some bullies are quite popular, particularly among their early adolescent classmates who see them as "cool" (Juvonen et al., 2003).

Bullies can attack their victims physically, verbally, or online. Cyberbullying has become so rampant in schools that of this writing all but six states have enacted antibullying laws (Engel & Sandstrom, 2010). Social networking has become a new medium for bullies (Shah, 2011b). They will also frequently manifest their behavior by shunning tactics that include not letting a student sit at a lunch table or ignoring certain classmates during sports events (Haber, 2007).

It has been reported by West (2009) that a study conducted over 2005/2006 by the National Institutes of Health noted the following trends:

- Verbal bullying (making fun of victims, teasing in a mean way, calling victims mean names, saying something nasty about a person's race or religion) was the most prevalent form of bulling;
- Boys are more likely to be involved in both physical (hitting, punching, pushing, shoving, kicking, and locking a victim somewhere in the school) and verbal bullying;
- Girls are more likely to ostracize their classmates or spread rumors;
- Most bullying occurs in middle school, particularly in seventh and eighth grades, and declines thereafter;
- Black adolescents, compared with whites, were more likely to be bullies, and correspondingly less likely to be victims;
- Hispanics, compared with whites, were more involved in physical bullying but were more likely to suffer cyberbullying.

The study also noted that the number of friends a student has was significant in determining hostile behavior. Students with many friends are at higher risk of becoming bullies; students with fewer friends are more often victims of bullies. Bullying is still so prevalent that the new Safe-School chief, Kevin Jennings, has made bullying his top concern (McNeil, 2009).

Engel & Sandstrom (2010) have concluded from their research that our students lack a sense of responsibility for each other's welfare. To address this void they recommend that schools "teach children how to be good to one another, how to cooperate, how to defend someone who is being picked on and how to stand up for what is right" (Engel & Sandstrom, p. A2).

If you employ the guidelines in this chapter to establish positive student relationships, these guidelines should address the above and will also work with bullies. Communicate to them positive expectations, show off their successes, and provide public and private recognition (Boynton & Boynton, 2005).

In particular, bullies generally have potential for leadership. However, the bully's leadership is distinguished from that of other students in his or her lack of empathy (Haber, 2007). The teacher should channel the potential leadership ability of the bully in a constructive direction by providing opportunities for management roles in the classroom such as leading discussions, tutoring other students, and assuming classroom responsibilities (Beane, 1999).

One principal wanted to change the school culture with regard to bullying. Fed up with hearing students calling each other names such as "Fag" and "Loser," she wanted to get her teachers to teach students to treat each other with respect by infusing compassion, tolerance, and decency into all classroom activities. To accomplish this she decided to use a structured, student-centered discussion about experiences with bullying when the "teachable moment" arrived (Shulkind, 2008).

> We knew we had been successful when Dillon, the coolest boy in the 8th grade, turned to Freddy, a socially awkward, stuttering peer, and said, "When I first got to this school, I was fat and wore thick glasses. All the kids were mean to me, and I used to sit alone at lunch every day." Dillon went on to explain that Freddy suggested they sit together, and it changed his entire middle school experience.
>
> Then, in front of incredulous teachers and fellow students, Dillon began to sob. And the room full of middle schoolers we so readily assume are insensitive, sat in a silent, respectful trance.
>
> Later that morning, I witnessed students surround Dillon in support. Some sat next to him. Some stroked his hand or wiped his tears. Some were the very same students involved in the bullying incidents that spurred these conversations in the first place. Brutish or tender—we get the behavior we expect. It's all in the messages we send, the attitudes we display, and the expectations we communicate. This scene is not pie-in-the-sky idealism. In fact, it's pragmatic. It's what you get when you teach kids, deliberately and explicitly, to care.

### *Are You an Educator or a Bully?*

Teachers who are bullies have no place in the twenty-first-century classroom. Starr (2003) identifies the attributes of teachers who are educators and those who are bullies.

> Educators let students know they care.
> Bullies let students know who's boss.
> Educators teach self-control.
> Bullies exert their own control.
> Educators set ironclad expectations.
> Bullies rule with whims of steel.
> Educators diffuse minor disruptions with humor.
> Bullies use sarcasm to turn disruptions into confrontations.
> Educators privately counsel chronic discipline problems.
> Bullies publicly humiliate chronic misbehavers.
> Educators are judicious
> Bullies are judgmental.
> Educators, aware of the power they wield over their students, choose their words and actions carefully.

Bullies wield their power recklessly, frequently resorting to anger and intimidation.
Educators help all students feel successful.
Bullies punish students for being unsuccessful.
Educators address misbehavior.
Bullies attack the character of the misbehavers.
Educators see each student's uniqueness.
Bullies compare children to one another.
Educators treat all students with respect.
Bullies make it clear that not all students deserve respect.
Educators highlight good behavior.
Bullies make examples of poor behavior.
Educators are proactive; they create classroom environments that minimize student misbehavior.
Bullies are reactive; they blame students for the lack of order in their classrooms.
Educators educate.
Bullies humiliate.
Educators exude confidence in their ability to maintain order in their classrooms.
Bullies barely conceal their terror of losing control.

You will note that most of the attributes of "Educators" have already been discussed so far in this book. Others will follow.

Finally, *videotape your class periodically*. It would be interesting for you and your students to observe how they interact with you and how they interact with each other. Spend some time first analyzing the tape yourself and then having the students analyze it so that you can elicit their reactions and recommendations for improvements.

In conclusion, Michael Anderson, a math teacher who had a disastrous first year, and eventually became his district's Teacher of the Year, finally came up with his recipe for a successful classroom. "Earn students' respect, create an environment where it's safe for them to try and even fail, and then make the material relevant to their lives" (Gammill, 2010).

## Summary: Establishing a Positive Classroom Atmosphere Regarding the Learning Environment

- Ensure a feeling of physical and emotional safety.
- Be enthusiastic.
- Prepare enough engaging activities to do when students complete tasks.
- Teach for success.
- Give students an occasional break.
- Ensure that you are connected with your students and they are connected with each other.

- Create an environment that is safe from bullies.
- Self-reflect periodically by audio- or video-recording your and your students' performance.

### Self-Reflection

What do you do to make students feel welcome?
What do you do to convey the responsibility of all students to make each other feel welcome?
How do you interact positively with your students?
How do you ensure that they interact positively with each other?
How enthusiastic are you? How do you show enthusiasm?
How do you teach so that all students will succeed?
Have you ever exhibited any of the attributes of bullies? If so, how could you have changed your behavior to display the corresponding attributes of an educator?

### Eliminating Teacher-Caused Student Misbehavior Problems

Consider behavior problems you witnessed in elementary, high school, and in the school where you are presently teaching that were actually caused by teachers. As you read this section, try to think of specific examples of teacher behaviors in each category presented that occurred in these classes and which of these behaviors are also bullying in nature. Reflect on how witnessing or being subjected to some of these behaviors made you feel and how you and/or other students reacted.

Some of these negative teacher behaviors that do not belong in a successful learning community include the following.

*Sarcasm and Ridicule.* You may recall being in a classroom where the teacher or other students made sarcastic remarks directed at you. Teachers who indulge in sarcasm, ridicule, or humiliation invite vindictive behavior from students, especially from students in middle or high school.

> Example: A teacher once said to one of his tenth-grade students, "You should see a witch doctor," and the student retorted, "When are your office hours?"

Some teachers may also try to get students to behave properly or do academic work using inappropriate remarks and/or name-calling such as, "When will you wake up?" "We've done this already, what's wrong with you?" or "Don't you get it yet, Dumbo?"

*Carrying a grudge.* If you have a negative encounter with a student, let the student know that *it is over* so that he can begin again.

Example: Jim "removed" some pens from the teacher's desk. The next time pens were missing, the teacher accused Jim of taking them, though he was innocent.

How do you think this accusation on the part of the teacher might affect Jim's future behavior? If the teacher, instead, had asked the entire class if anyone had "borrowed" the pens, this request would have shown Jim that he was not being charged unnecessarily.

Also, reaching out to a student with a note, phone call, or e-mail after a negative incident will go far in avoiding further unpleasant experiences (Canter & Canter, 2001).

Example: Mr. Wills sent this e-mail to his twelfth-grade student.

> Hi Hector,
> We had a disagreement today, but now it's over. Let's start again.
> Be sure to shake my hand when you come to class tomorrow. I look forward to it.
> Mr. Wills.

You can see how the tone of this message is conducive to a new beginning with the student.

*Favoritism.* Part of being human is that you have certain preferences. It is normal to like some students better than others. But few things turn off students more than teachers who show these preferences by having pets. In a twenty-first-century learning environment in which all members support each other, this behavior on the part of teachers is unacceptable.

Be aware of some behaviors that show preferences. Teachers who call on and praise the same students, smile at them exclusively, make them stars of class plays or monitors while ignoring other students, cause resentment. Remember that cooperation is your goal. You can likely identify from your past some teachers who favored certain students. Consider how these teachers demonstrated favoritism and how that behavior affected all students in the class.

*Making a case out of the most minor infraction, especially in the presence of others.*

> Example: Jenna is chewing gum. The teacher says, "Jenna, are you a baby who constantly needs something in your mouth? You'd be better off sucking your thumb." The class laughs.

Another version of making a case out of chewing gum occurs when the teacher addresses this "poem" to gum-chewing Jenna.

A gum-chewing girl,
And a cud-chewing cow,
What is the difference?
I know now,
The intelligent look on the face of the cow.

The entire matter might have been handled by a traditional teacher by saying to Jenna, "Put the gum in the waste basket." However, a contemporary classroom manager would first ask Jenna herself (and if there is no response, the class) if she had violated a rule, and if so, what *she* should do about it. Remember also that an effective twenty-first-century teacher would have made sure that rules are reasonable, agreed to, and accepted by all students. In this case, the core question would be if chewing gum is really a serious infraction worthy of a rule against it at all.

*Talking above students' voices while giving directions or conducting instruction.* A contemporary classroom manager wants to ensure that there is mutual respect among all class members. The teacher respects the students by listening to them when they speak; the students respect the teacher by listening when she speaks; the students respect each other by listening when they speak.

If there is not this cooperation, the teacher should determine why this is so. Are the students bored? Was their attention secured before the teacher or anyone else began to speak? Do the students understand the goals and objectives of instruction? Are there other underlying causes? The noise level in the classroom will intensify if you keep teaching or giving directions while the students are talking and not paying attention. But when students are actively engaged in productive group work, you can expect a reasonable noise level in the classroom.

*Employing top-down communication in your classroom instead of facilitating the free and open interchange of ideas and suggestions.* Authoritarian approaches to classroom management turn off students and have no place in the classroom of a contemporary manager. It was already indicated in chapter 1 that an authoritative as opposed to an authoritarian style is much more effective in dealing with students.

An authoritarian teacher makes all the rules with no input from students. An authoritative teacher establishes rules through discussion with students. While infractions are met with consequences, they are not punishing in nature. The authoritative style is characterized by warmth, consistency, and mutually discussed and selected rules and is the recommended style according to the research (Marzano, 2003).

*Setting up an instructional system involving rote learning, drudgery, lack of student participation, and lack of variety.* Be aware of instruction you provide that may involve these negative attributes. In addition to the fact that these negative approaches do not promote student achievement, students not engaged in meaningful activities will seek their own stimulation and find ways to become disruptive.

*Ignoring students' strengths and emphasizing failures.* Capitalizing on students' strengths leads to success. This success stimulates further motivation to achieve and reduces the desire for students to become disruptive.

> Teachers should be aware of the fact that students' belief systems can affect success or failure. If students believe that failing means they are stupid, they are likely to adopt many self-protective, but also self-defeating, strategies. Just telling students to "try harder" is not particularly effective. Students need real evidence that effort will pay off, that setting a higher goal will not lead to failure, that they can improve, and that abilities can be changed. They need authentic mastery experiences (Woolfolk, 2008, p. 431).

The above is a typical example of the strong connection between instruction and classroom management. The contemporary classroom manager helps students set instructional goals; demonstrates what goal mastery looks like; finds ways to demonstrate a student's progress; provides suggestions for improvement; emphasizes the link between past efforts and past accomplishments; and confronts directly self-defeating strategies (Woolfolk, 2008).

*Requiring busy work.* This type of assignment is unproductive and particularly irking to students, especially when the busy work, or any other assignment for that matter, is not returned. Teachers should constantly reflect on their assignments to make sure that they are meaningful.

*Giving the same activities and assignments to all students instead of being selective according to need.* Students who have instructional and procedural assignments that will tend to lead to success have fewer opportunities to become off-task and disruptive.

*Inconsistency.* Some teachers are inconsistent in implementing procedures. Sometimes teachers will allow calling out; other times they will insist that hands be raised. It becomes confusing to students when teachers do not enforce rules and procedures in the same way all the time.

Being consistent, insistent, and persistent makes students feel secure (Canter, 2006). They know what to expect when a question is asked, when they have to ask permission to perform a certain activity, and how to complete assignments. Schools that experience *discipline* problems do so when rules are unclear, perceived by students as unfair, or not believed in by students; misconduct is ignored; teachers/administrators do not know or disagree about rules; and teachers' attitudes tend to be punitive (Washburn et al., 2007).

It should be noted that consistency does *not* mean inflexibility. As stated earlier, there may be times when you need to reflect on procedures and change, with student input, those that may not be effective.

## Summary: Teacher-Caused Student Misbehavior

- Sarcasm
- Carrying a grudge
- Favoritism
- Making a case out of minor infractions
- Employing authoritarian approaches
- Ignoring students' strengths
- Not having students engaged in meaningful activities
- Assigning busy work
- Being inconsistent

## Self-Reflection

How have you used student strengths in your classroom?

If you ever had an altercation with a student, how did you follow through?

What evidence can you give that your classroom activities and assignments are meaningful?

How consistent are you in implementing rules and procedures?

Have you ever been sarcastic with a student? If so, what was the result?

Which students do you tend to like more? Have you ever done anything to show your preferences? Have your students ever indicated to you orally, in writing, or through gestures that you have preferences?

Have you ever made a big deal out of a minor situation?

Have you ever said (or thought), "Do it because I said so"?

# 3
# Reactive Approaches to Classroom Management

EVEN THOUGH YOU MAY HAVE EXHAUSTED ALL PREVENTIVE MEASURES, classroom misbehavior problems will still occur. How you handle misbehavior once it does occur is important in avoiding its recurrence.

When dealing with misbehavior, it does not necessarily mean that you must discard all of the old ways, but that you examine them and build on those that are positive. Always remember that, as a contemporary classroom manager, whenever possible, your reaction to behavior problems should be *educative* and should reinforce current recommended practices.

### Educational Intervention Techniques for Handling Student Misbehavior

As stated previously, student ownership of all phases of managing the classroom offers the key to success. Effective practices in fostering this ownership consist of student input; shared responsibility; student autonomy, control, and involvement; self-regulation; and self-reflection. In addition, whenever misbehavior occurs, you should immediately analyze whether the students involved understand their role in a positive and supportive classroom environment and the goals/objectives of instruction, and whether they are engaged in meaningful activities. Following are methods for handling misbehavior problems.

*Emphasize positive behavior.* You may emphasize positive behavior in several ways. Contrast the following two teacher statements addressed to Nicole and Martha regarding *Nicole's* misbehavior, which in this case is not paying attention.

> Statement 1: "Nicole, stop fiddling with your makeup case and pay attention."
> Statement 2: "Martha, I like the way you're paying attention and ready for the lesson."

In the first statement the teacher tells Nicole how to behave. In the second statement, the teacher rewards (praises) Martha's positive behavior in the attempt to alert Nicole to the behavior she is supposed to be demonstrating. Even though Statement 2 is more effective than Statement 1, it is a traditional approach. Note that in addition to praise, the teacher is also using an "I" message in which he is exercising control.

There are some educators who believe that praise as used above is judgmental and can be problematic (Kohn, 1993, 2001; Tauber, 1999). They see praise as manipulative. It is something teachers do to students to get them to cooperate rather than engage them in a discussion of more important topics such as what makes a good classroom work well or how what they do or neglect to do affects other class members.

Praise may increase students' dependence on the teacher, may cause students to lose interest, and as a result, reduce achievement. Using too much praise is ineffective in getting students to become self-managed because it informs the students that they should behave properly not for their own sake but to please you. However, Dreikurs (1998) promoted the practice of praising *effort* rather than performance because effort is within the student's control, whereas physical dexterity and innate ability that could lead to higher performance levels are not.

A different way of emphasizing positive behavior is through *behavioral narration* in which you state the behavior of students who are complying with rules and/or procedures (Canter, 2006). Behavioral narration is *descriptive*. In Statement 2 above, you would use behavioral narration to describe what Martha is doing. "Martha is paying attention and ready for the lesson." Another example is, "Juanita has cleared her desk and her eyes are on me."

Yet another way to highlight the positive is by stating the behavior the misbehaving student *should* be demonstrating. It is more useful to make a positive statement such as, "Hank, your pad should be away," instead of making a negative statement such as, "Don't doodle during class."

A more contemporary approach to dealing with Hank's misbehavior is to ask him, "What are you doing to prevent our class from making progress?" He might answer, "I should put my pad away" or "I should stop doodling."

Whenever possible, your reaction should aim at increasing student responsibility. It is best to remind students of rules *they* have participated in constructing (assuming that you have done so at the beginning of the school year), have the students decide which rules are not being followed, and then what to do about it.

> Example: "Louis, look at the rule chart our class came up with and tell me which one you are now violating to hold up the class." Or you could simply have Louis just verbalize what he is doing to hold up the class. "I should clear my desk."

You might also point to the rule as you continue instruction without interruption.

*State positive outcomes for correcting the misbehavior.* When the student behaves appropriately, there will be a positive result.

> Example: "When you get back into your seat, Georgette, it will be your turn to guide our Smartboard."
>
> "When you get back into your seat, Georgette, our class will be able to continue to work on the projects they enjoy."

*Request that a student state or put in writing what current misbehavior he or she is demonstrating.* Some students are unaware that they are misbehaving (Glasser, 1975). Stating or writing the misbehavior brings it to a student's consciousness so that he or she can then correct the misbehavior.

> Example: "What are you doing, Jack?"
> At first Jack might say, "Uh, nothing"
> Then you would ask the question again. "What are you doing, Jack?"
> "I am poking Juan."
> "What should you be doing?"
> "I should be paying attention."

*Rearrange seating.* If you find that some students have become overfriendly in class, break up the seating pattern. If the students have become overfriendly while working in groups, change the group structure. Twenty-first-century classroom managers know that noncompliance is a symptom. You will want to *analyze* why that symptom is occurring and what can be done to remedy the situation.

*Remain calm.* Quietly remind the class or a particular student that work is being held up. Avoid yelling (Tate, 2007). Yelling tells students that you are out of control, that you have "lost your cool." There are some students who enjoy getting the teacher to this state, and if you show you have reached it, they will repeat the same pattern that reinforces *your* behavior. The angrier a student becomes the calmer you need to be. Your calmness serves as a stimulus that will help calm his or her anger (MacKenzie, 1996).

It is difficult but imperative to maintain emotional objectivity. To keep this objectivity at a high level, the teacher should avoid finger pointing, ridiculing, glaring at, or hovering over the offending student as well as raising the tone of voice with him or her. These behaviors should be replaced with keeping an appropriate distance from the student, speaking directly to him or her in a respectful way, looking directly without staring, and exhibiting a neutral or positive facial expression (Marzano, 2007).

Another related point is to avoid arguments with students. If you make the students the enemy, they will win (Rigsbee, 2008). When arguments occur, the class should first decide how to handle them. Assuming that their decision is reasonable, you should abide by it. Here again, you could ask the misbehaving student what he should be doing. You could also just stand firm and keep repeating *calmly* the behavior you want a student to demonstrate until he does so (Walker et al., 2004). "Carlos, sit down and open your book." "Carlos, sit down and open your book," "Carlos, sit down and open your book."

*Keep the flow of the lesson while making minor corrections.* You want to keep the momentum going by avoiding unnecessary interruptions thus providing a cause for more disruptions. The more subtle your reaction, the better the chance that you will not have breaks in instruction.

> Examples: Call on a student who is not paying attention. You should do this in a nonthreatening way as a casual reminder that she is supposed to be paying attention.
>
> Use the student's name in context during the lesson. Read the following approaches:
>
> "Maureen, it's time for you to listen."
>
> "When we analyzed this problem yesterday, Maureen, we came up with some criteria."

In the second approach you reminded Maureen to pay attention without losing the momentum or content of the lesson.

*Keep in physical contact with everyone in the class.* Some teachers seem to be glued to the front of the room, especially during whole class instruction. They remain in the same position during the lesson, often standing at the board. Group focus, the suggestion of Kounin (1970) that you read earlier to prevent behavior problems, can also be used once they occur. Anticipate where trouble is brewing by moving to that section of the room. Conduct the class there for a while; then move to another area.

If a lot of board work is required during the lesson, train students to do some of the writing for you, leaving you free to move about, or prepare overheads or PowerPoint displays in advance and let the students operate the equipment at your direction as you circulate around the room.

If a student is playing with an object on the desk, move over to that student, *gently* remove the object from his/her hand and put it where it belongs while keeping the discussion going. This technique is more successful than interrupting the lesson to say, "Doreen, put that eraser away."

*If a student or students begin speaking while you are speaking, interrupt your sentence during a word at the end of a syl . . .*

Did that just get your attention?

Silence is likely to follow stopping your sentence in the middle of a word (at the end of a syllable). Silence is a powerful attention getter, and once you have that silence, you can continue speaking. This approach is more subtle and effective than stopping the lesson and saying, "Will everyone stop talking and pay attention?" Another approach is to keep talking and gradually lower your voice.

*As a shared leader in a learning community, you can express YOUR feeling about a misbehavior.* A specific type of "I" message introduced by Gordon (1974) is still being used today to communicate effectively your feelings to misbehaving students. This specific "I" message is different from the one previously introduced in chapter 2. Gordon's message has three parts. It states what the misbehavior is, the tangible effect that misbehavior has on you, and how it makes you feel.

> Examples: "When you call out answers (misbehavior), it makes it difficult for me to keep everyone in the class involved (effect on you), and I feel disappointed that I'm not doing my job properly (how you feel)."
>
> "When you keep taking pencils from my desk (misbehavior), I can't keep track of how many I have for the other students (effect on you), and I feel frustrated (how you feel)."

A modification of the above "I" message was offered by Canter & Canter (1992). They suggested that the "I" message be reversed. The Canters' version begins with the teacher's feeling, then the misbehavior, and finally what behavior the teacher wants instead.

> Example: "I feel I'm not doing my job properly (teacher's feeling) when you call out answers (misbehavior), and I want you to raise your hand if you want to participate in the discussion" (behavior the teacher wants).

This "I" message can be more in keeping with contemporary approaches by saying, "I feel I'm not doing my job properly (teacher's feeling) when you call out answers (misbehavior), and as the class decided, you should raise your hand if you want to participate in the discussion (behavior agreed to by both class and teacher).

Remember that when using "You" messages (referred to in table 2.1), the student's behavior is being reinforced. When using "I" messages, you are correcting misbehavior by expressing your feelings.

*Use nonverbal communication to keep students' attention.* Direct eye contact with a student will redirect his attention. While conducting the lesson you could also keep looking (not staring) at a student who is not looking at you or behaving appropriately. The other students are likely to signal the student that you are looking, which in turn should alert him to refocus attention on work.

You could turn off or flicker (once) the lights, or ring a bell to regain attention. Raising your hand, your brow, nodding or shaking your head, or placing your finger over your lips may also help. With younger children you can use the game, Statue, and say, "Freeze." Students at early grade levels respond well to this command.

You could also begin clapping in a different rhythm each time you want attention. Advise, teach, and practice with the students in advance so that whenever you do this, they should stop whatever they are doing, listen to the rhythm, and clap in the same rhythm. However, whichever stimulus you choose should be *varied*, for if you repeat the same stimulus constantly, the students will become conditioned to it and eventually ignore it.

At this point it would be suitable to reinforce the fact that only about 7 percent of communication comes through the spoken word. Body gestures, voice tone, facial expressions, and general posture communicate the rest. These nonverbal messages mean different things to students from different cultures, especially when there is a non-match between the spoken word and the body language. Since eye contact, gestures, physical proximity, as well as physical contact are interpreted differently, you must learn as much as you can about the various cultures represented in your class and act accordingly (McGee, 2008).

*Have individual conferences with students who are constantly behaving improperly.* If you make a case of students' misbehavior in front of the class, you may reinforce the misbehavior. Class members behave very differently individually from the way they do in groups. Students, adolescents in particular, try to maintain a high social status with their peers, making them defensive and creating difficulty for you to discover what the problem actually is.

Plan your conference by carefully structuring the questions you want to ask. Some examples are: "Is there anything I am doing that causes you to react the way you do in class?" "Is there a way I could improve the class to make it more interesting for you?" "Are you having a problem I could help you with?"

Sometimes asking the student to state if *you* are doing something to cause the misbehavior can be revealing. The student could be surprised that you asked the question, and may realize for the first time that her behavior is affecting you. The student may actually tell you if you are doing something that bothers her and may suggest other topics of interest, and/or other ways of learning or being evaluated.

Just as people who work in industry recognize that sharing ideas over a business lunch improves communication with customers and increases sales, sharing a one-to-one meal with a chronically misbehaving student can promote a more positive relationship with that student and foster improved cooperation on her part.

*Apply logical consequences.* In keeping with making the students responsible for their own behavior, it is an effective procedure to apply logical consequences for misbehavior (Glasser, 1975). Logical consequences are educative. They are not the same as punishment because they are directly connected to the misbehavior and hold the student accountable while maintaining his dignity (Gootman, 1997).

Logical consequences should not be packaged as logical consequences but should be *really* logical (Kohn, 1996). They should have some conceptual connection to the student's behavior.

> Examples: A student who punches another student (misbehavior) must make a list of alternative ways to settle disputes (logical consequence).
>
> A student who draws graffiti on a wall (misbehavior) must clean it (logical consequence).

*Use peers to correct misbehavior.* Try to keep the level of engagement and motivation so high in your classroom that the other students themselves will tend to correct the disrupters. This approach will be more successful if students have been empowered to share responsibility with you for instruction and for classroom management. Whenever possible, have the students decide what to do about a person who is (constantly) disrupting the class. (See "The Classroom Meeting" in chapter 10.)

An effective variation of using peers is using reverse modeling. Have a student who is misbehaving model the *correct* behavior for the other students.

> Example "Harry (the student who is fooling around instead of getting ready to leave), show the class what to do to get ready for dismissal."

## More Challenging Cases

There will always be some behavioral situations that will be more challenging. Some specific strategies (systems) for dealing with these challenges will be presented in part 2.

In chapter 1 you read that some behavioral challenges involved moral issues, aggression/violence, and gang membership. You were advised that some situations may not be conducive to handling them by yourself and that you might have to seek the help of a specialist. You were also informed that misbehavior was symptomatic and that the *only* exception where a student could not control behavior involved organic disorders. Now that you have read some of the ways to deal with misbehavior problems, consider how a caring classroom atmosphere in which students interact with each other and with other students positively might have prevented aggressive behaviors from reaching that stage.

The National Education Association reports other demanding situations on their website (www.nea.org). These include dealing with the class clown, recalcitrant students, and with fighting students. Remember, once again, that these disruptive behaviors will have much less of an opportunity to flourish if you have built a sense of community in your class. As you read through the following section, *think of how the following occurrences (symptoms) could be avoided or at least mitigated if students in your class support and feel responsible for each other.*

*The class clown.* This student uses joking as an attention-seeking device. In many cases he is successful and this success serves as a stimulant for further clowning. As a twenty-first-century classroom manager, first ask yourself why this behavior is occurring. How involved is this student? How successful is he? What can be done to improve his achievement?

Then ask the class for their input by saying, "We have decided to achieve these goals together. How is _____ interfering with our success?" "How is _____'s behavior interfering with his success?" Then, "What is the best way to deal with this situation?" Assuming that the class cannot handle this behavior, the NEA suggests that you could without direct eye contact approach the student who is clowning and warn him about possible isolation. If the warning does not stop the misbehavior, move the student to a different part of the classroom for a brief time.

*Recalcitrant students.* If a student is noncompliant, the teacher should analyze why the student is refusing to do the assigned work. If the class cannot help solve the situation, try doing some of the work with the student. While working together, the NEA recommends that you discuss the assignment to see if the student understands it and can find some motivation in it. Remind the student of similar (or any) assignments in which she experienced success. If necessary, have the student select a different task with a similar goal or objective before returning to the original assignment.

At any sign of beginning the assignment, offer the student encouragement. Communicate high expectations for effort by saying something similar to: "Rule number one is that everyone must participate. That means one hundred percent. The reason our class set up this rule is that the more we participate, the more we achieve. We don't use words such as *can't* or *won't*. At least try, and if you need help, you'll get it" (National Education Association, 2009).

*Students involved in fights.* Sometimes students have arguments that can accelerate into fights. Some basic techniques for breaking up fights and dealing with physically aggressive students are offered by Johns & Carr (1995). They suggest that small acts of aggression can escalate into more violent acts. Therefore, do not ignore aggression.

Since frequently the mere presence of an adult will stop a potentially violent act, move toward the violent scene. Review the situation quickly to determine who is involved and what may likely happen.

If gangs are involved, send a nonparticipant for more adults. Check for weapons. Because students sometimes hope that an adult will tell them to stop fighting to give them a "graceful" way to bow out, tell students in a strong voice to stop. Tell onlookers to leave. Make a mental note of the onlookers. If you know any of these observers by name, address them *by name* and tell them where to go.

Inform observers and those involved in the fighting of the consequences of not following your directions. *Never* get in between fighting students. Tell the students to stop in a loud, demanding voice remembering that many times students will welcome an excuse to quit. When the incident is over, document what happened and share this information with others, as required. Most important, as soon as possible after the incident is over, get professional help for both victims and aggressors.

## Handling Student Misbehavior

- Emphasize positive behavior.
- Ask the student to state or write the current misbehavior.
- Rearrange seating.
- Remain calm.
- Keep the momentum of the lesson while correcting minor misbehavior.
- Keep in proximity with all students.
- Use silence to recapture student attention.
- Express your feelings about a student's misbehavior.
- Use gestures to keep student attention.
- Schedule individual conferences with chronically misbehaving students.
- Apply logical consequences.
- Use peers to correct misbehavior.

If all of the proactive and reactive suggestions you have read seem overwhelming to you, be confident in the fact that implementing successful classroom management is an art that incorporates many different strategies and, as with all other skills, takes *time* to master. The more you practice these strategies in your classroom, the more adept you will be at recognizing when they will be effective and how to apply them.

Also, remember that we are in an era of shared leadership and responsibility with students. "In the end, experts say that teachers can only *influence* (italics in original) behavior; the rest is up to the student . . . [for] systems—not teachers—change student behavior (Franklin, 2006). You will review some of these systems in part 2.

**Punishment: Is It Necessary?**

Punishment is a result (penalty) following a response (misbehavior) that decreases the chances that the misbehavior will be repeated. Schools (and teachers) have frequently responded to punitive approaches that have limited value (Osher et al., 2010).

It is, therefore, helpful to distinguish between two types of punishment: contrived and naturally occurring (Cangelosi, 2008). A contrived punishment has no relation to the misbehavior. A naturally occurring punishment is a normal and practical consequence of the misbehavior.

> Example: Melinda is fooling around in math class.
> Contrived punishment: She is not allowed to go to recess or she is assigned to detention.
> Naturally occurring punishment: She fails the math test or gets a lower grade than she could have achieved.

The latter (naturally occurring) situation is that which was referred to earlier in this chapter as a logical consequence. Logical consequences, as opposed to punishments, intend to teach; foster internal locus of control (behavior control within the student); are proactive, logical, and related to the misbehavior; and work in the long term (Curwin and Mendler, 1999, 2008). There are many educators who do not consider these types of consequences to be punishments at all. The confusion between contrived and naturally occurring punishment may be one reason why the research on punishment is sometimes conflicting.

Logical consequences should not be packaged as logical consequences but should be *really* logical and not merely "punishment-light" Kohn (1996) warns. He believes that some "logical" consequence force students into compliance as opposed to committing themselves to what they are doing, developing deep understanding of their misbehavior, and considering what kind of people would want to act that way.

Kohn (1996) goes on to say that this lack of understanding occurs when teachers are in complete control of the classroom and when they do not persistently ask themselves when students do not comply if there is the possibility that the actual problem may be with what the students have been asked to do or learn.

In general, there are two methods for inflicting punishment: removing a reward, or imposing an aversive stimulus—one that is irritating or unpleasant. The former is the preferred method. It may take the form of simply removing a student from the group as in time-out, or withholding an activity the student might enjoy such as participating in a field trip or in a game. As suggested earlier, whenever appropriate, the student should *verbalize or write* what misbehavior is causing him or her to be removed from the group.

Remember that isolating students can be a reward for those who do not wish to work or are seeking attention from their peers. Be sure that the rewards students receive are in the classroom group, not in the time-out section of the room (Wolfgang, 2005).

It should be noted that Kohn (2005) has indicated that in his research, time-out had a damaging effect of love withdrawal. He found that parents (and by inference, teachers) who relied more on warmth and reason as opposed to control with procedures such as time-out were more likely to have students who complied and who developed into responsible, compassionate, and mentally healthy people.

Contrived punishments are almost always defined by the school district, but also the conditions under which they will be inflicted. Normally, a team makes the decision, not the individual teacher, though the teacher can bring up the situation for discussion. Serious infractions such as stealing, drug dealing, or violent behavior causing physical harm to others are generally examples of conditions that trigger contrived punishments.

Before being willing to recommend the need for a contrived punishment, a teacher should do some serious self-reflection to see if he or she has used proactive measures, avoided self-caused problems, and implemented reactive educational interventions, especially logical consequences, all of which were described previously. Contrived punishment should be assigned when the misbehavior is consistent, not the first time or two a student misbehaves.

Sometimes ignoring the misbehavior will not reinforce it, especially when the student misbehaves deliberately to seek attention. A student to whom punishment will be administered should be warned beforehand. And when action is finally taken, it should focus on students' inappropriate behavior rather than on their histories or personalities (Cotton, 2000).

When punishment becomes absolutely necessary, and, as previously stated, this situation is usually described by the school district, it is imperative to remember that the punishment should be related and proportional to the misbehavior. The old adage, "Let the punishment fit the crime," should be applied.

Always document any serious acts. When punishment is administered following these acts, it should be done calmly. This is a time a teacher and/or team need to keep their wits about them so that they can select punishment rationally. Remember that the type of punishment must be approved as such in school guidelines. To be effective, punishment should be imposed as soon as possible after the misbehavior so that there is a connection between the misbehavior and its consequences.

Imposing punishment is not a pleasant act for teachers and a choice they prefer to avoid. But for those who advocate no contrived or naturally occurring punishment ever, Marzano (2003) has countered that an overwhelming body of research does not support that conclusion, supporting instead "a balanced approach that employs a variety of techniques" (p. 28).

### Self-Reflection

What types of misbehavior are most frequently demonstrated in your classroom?

How do you usually handle these misbehaviors?

How successful were you in dealing with these misbehaviors?

How might you change the ways you have dealt with misbehaviors to reflect a more contemporary approach?

# 4

# Being Thorough When Considering Other Management Factors in Your Classroom

IN A SUCCESSFUL TWENTY-FIRST-CENTURY CLASSROOM, there are several other factors teachers must consider when managing their classrooms. These are time, grouping, and assisting students in self-direction.

## Managing Time

For a classroom to run smoothly, a teacher has to be able to manage time. Cotton (1990) estimated that classroom time spent on instruction is slightly more than half, with the remainder spent on misbehavior problems. This is an enormous waste, especially since *the amount of time spent on teaching is directly correlated with student achievement* (Rosenshine, 1979; Karweit, 1988).

In your own years as a student, think of how much classroom time was wasted—time that could have been better spent on your learning. As a teacher, you should spend more time to save time. There are several ways to accomplish this.

- Observe the sequence of normal daily activities and identify each. Establish a system that is comfortable for you for *every activity* in the classroom, including acquiring and storing materials, controlling inventory, planning effective lessons, dealing with attendance, delegating chores, accommodating for missed learning when students are absent or out of class, and shifting from one activity to another (transitions).

- Teach your students to set goals as well as timely methods for achieving them. Share with students how you set goals, and what you do to make sure they are attained.
- Ask the students for their input regarding how time may be used more productively. Raising this time-saving idea to their consciousness will help them become more aware of ways to become more efficient.
- Use differences in learners as a time-saving asset as opposed to a liability. Establishing a system for students' checking their own work and for checking each other's not only saves time but also helps create independence.
- As with successful managers in all areas, do not hesitate to delegate. To do this you must first have faith that some activities can be delegated. Then you must clearly identify which tasks can be delegated, and which cannot. Determine which resource people you will need, and teach them how to implement the procedures you want.

It should be pointed out that the school staffs have indicated that the most difficult time they have with student behavior is during transitions, especially when changing activities (National Education Association, n.d.). Transitions problems would be minimized if the class had input regarding how to move to different activities without disruptions.

To ensure that students change activities efficiently, cue the students verbally ahead of time (perhaps five minutes) that a transition is coming and what behavior you are looking for. When the time actually comes, signal with a bell, rhythmic clapping of hands, playing music, or other signal you deem appropriate (Wong & Wong, 2005). Compliment students who are cooperating with your transition expectations. Be sure to have the next assignment ready for the students to begin. When all the students are in place in their new setting, give another signal that it is time to begin.

## Managing Groups

A classroom that is flexible enough to meet the needs of all students will provide time for group work. In order to have group work flow efficiently, there are several decisions a teacher must make. But before any final decisions are made, it should be repeated here that just as students should provide input into rules, procedures, and other classroom management decisions, students should also participate in helping determine group procedures (Stefanou et al., 2004).

These decisions might include the following: When two or more groups are working simultaneously, where should they be located? How will transitions be made from one activity to another? What procedure(s) should be set up for moving from one group to another, or from moving from one group before another can move?

To manage groups more effectively, once the agreed-upon procedures have been adopted:

- Make sure that the procedures for moving in and out of groups are clear. Have the students restate, especially in their own words, the procedures. Then *rehearse* them, not just once but several times.
- Identify groups by names, colors, or numerals according to what is age appropriate.
- Post clear directions to remind students what to do as soon as they get into a group.
- Inform students that each is responsible for his or her own work but may ask another member of the group for help if it is needed. That student must give help. The teacher can be asked for help only if everyone in the group agrees on the same question.
- As in conducting any lesson, have enough for students to do when they complete a task.
- Decide how frequently and at what point groups will be monitored.
- Use resources such as teacher assistants; parents; student teachers; and college and high school student observers. Ask for their input and suggestions, as well as recommendations from your own students, regarding how their mutually decided group procedures can improve so that these procedures can be more effective.

### Assisting Students in Self-Direction

You have already read several times in this book that students should participate in establishing rules and procedures. You should also consider how to assist students in monitoring their own behavior. This task can be approached in the following ways:

- Once you have taught students to set their own goals and standards, and timely methods for achieving them, help the students determine when the goals have been achieved.
- Help students decide what behavior is appropriate and inappropriate as well as what consequences misbehavior will have. Students should understand why the misbehavior is inappropriate and what effect it has on them and on others.

- Support students in developing the attitude that helping each other is rewarding. Have them keep diaries where they reflect on their own behavior, identifying when the behavior was productive, when it impeded their progress, and what they could do about it. Read the diaries periodically and return them with comments.
- Have students practice proper behavior that you model for them.

As stated earlier, you should remember that even though your ultimate goal is having students manage their own behavior, you are ultimately responsible for the behavior of *all* students in your classroom (Canter, 2006).

### Self-Reflection

How do you manage time efficiently so that more of it can be spent on learning?

What procedures and processes involved in group work have you and your students set up together?

How have you assisted your students in becoming self-directed?

# 5

# Maximizing Preparation for the Opening of School

B[EFORE THE NEXT SCHOOL YEAR BEGINS]{.smallcaps}, it would be more than worth your while to invest time *rethinking* very carefully how to organize your classroom, and what procedures you will want to have in place the first day of school. The investment will pay off in dividends that will make your life and that of your students much easier and less stressful.

> Each school year, the first couple of days are crucial for setting the pace for the entire year. It's very important for the teacher and students to have a mental map of how the coming year should look, as well as a set of guiding principles and rules that they will follow. In a nutshell, the class must create its own culture. (Damani, 2011, p. 1)

## Taking Action Ahead of Time

Think about how neat you keep your classroom (office, room, house). In a study conducted in the Netherlands, it was reported that when public areas were kept neat, citizens were less likely to make a mess (Schmid, 2008). This relationship is likely transferable to the classroom where students may keep the room neater, if you do so. Moreover, keeping your room neat eliminates a lot of chaos that could lead to class disruptions.

There are several procedures for you to consider. Obtain your schedule and, if you teach elementary grades, the schedules of your students to determine when they will be out of the room for special subjects or other planned instructional activities. Gather information about your students, especially information about those who may have special needs. Obtain any keys you will need for doors, closets, or lockers and *test the keys*.

Make sure that you are fully aware of and review the policy and procedures for requesting classroom repairs, accessing materials and supplies, completing paperwork required of you, reporting illness and accidents, releasing students early, admitting students who are tardy, passing through the halls, going to the lunch room, implementing fire drills, and dismissing students.

**Managing the Physical Plant**

In order to engage your students, you will have to consider what accommodations you want your classroom to provide. Cangelosi (2004) offered a set of criteria that one teacher, Ms. Del Rio, made to guide her classroom arrangement.

1. Quick and easy access for her between any two points in the room
2. A designated quiet area for students to engage in individualized work
3. A designated large group activity area for an entire class to congregate for discussions, lectures, tutorial sessions, and media presentations
4. Small group activity areas for cooperative groups to conduct their business
5. Storage space for equipment and materials to be kept out of sight
6. A secure teacher's desk in a location with a favorable vantage point
7. A silent reading room and mini-library that can comfortably accommodate several students at a time
8. A time-out room for isolating students
9. A private room in which Ms. Del Rio can hold uninterrupted conferences with individuals . . . when a class is not in session
10. A two-way communication device . . . with which she can quickly summon backup support in crisis situations (Cangelosi, 2004, p. 272).

You may find some or all of the above criteria important and/or you may want to add your own. But before you can organize or reorganize your classroom you must first review what in the room is permanent and what can be changed.

There are several fixed architectural features of the room. These include the locations of closets, doors, windows, running water, blackboards, electrical outlets, and built-in shelves; the room size, and a lavatory (for classrooms with very young students).

Other features can be altered. These include where you locate desks (unless you are working in a classroom where desks are still bolted to the floor), work stations, rug areas, bulletin boards, bookcases, pencil sharpeners, and wastepaper baskets.

The next consideration in setting up your classroom should be your students' needs. In providing instructional flexibility you will most likely have areas where students can work in large groups, small groups of three to six, pairs, or individually.

You must also decide where you will locate computers, software, manipulative material, and equipment. You have to consider how you will eliminate potential distractions. If you are sharing your room (when instruction is departmentalized) with another or other teachers, what accommodations will you need to make? Also, decide what effective educational use you can make out of your ceiling.

Safety factors are critically important too. Have you planned your room so that aisles are wide and will be clear? Is your equipment stored in areas that are off-limits to students unless being used? Will the students be sitting away from doors? Will electrical cords be connected and routed in a way that will prevent students from tripping? Will you be able to see where the students are at any one moment? How will you arrange to keep sharp or other dangerous objects out of younger or potentially violent students' reach?

If you conduct a laboratory course, what safety procedures will you teach your students? As with other procedural (and instructional) decisions, whatever you arrange originally can be changed upon recommendations of the students.

To keep the classroom moving smoothly, other organizational suggestions have been offered by George (2008).

1. Have specific places for students to turn in work. Using plastic stackable baskets with bold clear labels for each class period facilitates students' handing in their work.
2. Have a designated place for absent students to collect work. Place the corresponding assignment(s) with the student's name in a basket labeled "Absent Work" and the class period. This procedure puts the responsibility on the student to obtain the assignment from the basket and complete it.
3. Have a "No Name" folder. When students find that they are missing an assignment, ask if they have checked the No Name folder.
4. Use an online grading program. This makes it possible to share grades and other information with parents and students and saves a lot of time with fewer parent phone calls, fewer students questioning their grades, and less time preparing missing assignments. Most important, you will find yourself more accountable when grades are posted for parents and students to view.

5. Have a board in the hall outside your classroom where you write what students need for class each period. This reminder helps teach students to be organized, especially when they have to move from class to class.
6. Write the day's lesson topic for each class period on the board. This focuses both you and your students to the task at hand, helps students who may have to miss class know what they have to make up, and assists them in assuming responsibility and planning ahead.
7. Expect students to come to class prepared. Do not allow students to leave the room to get materials or equipment. Have a "What Do I Need for Class?" list for the day's lesson and the next day's lesson. The onus is then on the students to check the list and bring what they need to class because they know in advance that they will not go wandering around attempting to collect materials.
8. Keep seating charts handy. This will allow you to take attendance quickly as students complete a class starter assignment. The list is also valuable for substitute teachers.
9. Use e-mail for parent contacts whenever possible. This process is a time saver and makes it easy to keep a "paper" trail. When you notice something positive about a student (and you should go out of your way to find something) be sure to e-mail the parent. Accumulating positives will go a long way to ease subsequent behavior problems if they should subsequently occur.
10. Let go of the things that don't really matter. Reflect on your procedures or details that you require which may be time-consuming and not really worth the effort. (Adapted from George, 2008, by permission of the author.)

## The First Day(s) of School

It is a truism to state that you do not get a second chance to make a first impression. So if there was ever an event that deserves planning ahead, it is the first day of school. The first day and following weeks set the tone for the entire school year. It is a time when students are assessing you as much as you are assessing them.

Keep in mind that you should arrive on time, preferably *early* each day. As the students enter your classroom they are carrying articles of clothing, writing pads and utensils, and backpacks. Where are these materials to be placed? Do you have a row of lockers outside your classroom, in the classroom, or do you have just plain clothing hooks? Do you assign lockers or have the students select them?

Some teachers play classical music as their students enter the class and also during lessons. It has been reported that whenever classical music is played, students keep their noise levels lower than the sound of the music (Wong & Wong, 2005).

It would be best to stand at the door and greet each student not only the first day but *every* day by making a comment to each such as, "Hello," "Nice shirt," "Hi," and while doing so maintaining direct eye contact with each person. These are acts of acknowledgment and recognition and students behave differently when they know they are recognized. Then seat the students in a preplanned seating arrangement you have prepared for them.

Introduce yourself *briefly*. Share something about yourself with the students, perhaps something related to where you went to school, how you became interested in teaching, if you are married, have children, but *do not overdo the information*, especially the personal information.

Students are curious about what they will be doing in your class during the year. After you introduce yourself, spend a *short* amount of time describing what topics you and they will be covering and some instructional methods you will be offering.

For age-appropriate students have an interesting but brief activity they can immediately begin working on already written on the board. The activity should be something personal similar to, "The Five Most Important Things You Should Know about Me." As the students are completing the activity, you can begin taking the attendance. Do so quickly without dragging out the process.

If you are not absolutely sure how to pronounce a student's name, ask the student to pronounce it for you. If you say it incorrectly, you will provide the students, who are likely to know the person whose name you called, the opportunity to laugh and become disruptive.

Immediately after taking the attendance, set up the rules with input from the students (Wong & Wong, 1998, 2004). As a partner in classroom management, decide in advance what rules *you* want. Then conduct a brief discussion asking students for their input.

Phrase your discussion questions so that you will have the students tell you what is proper. For example, if you ask, "How should we behave?" the question is too vague and may lead to myriad answers. But if you say, "When we have a discussion or lesson, what should we do to make sure that everyone has an equal opportunity to be heard?" this question will likely give you the desired response, which is, "Raise your hand." You can then proceed to write on a chart, "Raise your hand to ask or answer a question."

You could also elicit the same result by having your students role-play a discussion or lesson in which there are no rules. The chaos that will likely ensue will give the students an opportunity to analyze the result and then offer a better way to behave during these activities. When all classroom rules are elicited, invest time in ensuring that the rules are understood, accepted, and practiced so that they become habitual (Evertson & Weinstein, 2006).

Display the rule chart in a visible place to serve as a reminder to everyone, and to provide a reference for rule breakers. You may also want to provide a set of those rules (laminated) for each student. If a student calls out an answer during your lesson, all you have to do without breaking the flow is continue your lesson while pointing to the rule. In the past a teacher might also say, "Raise your hand to ask or answer a question is the rule our class decided to follow."

While this approach would be acceptable, a contemporary classroom manager would more likely say to the offending student, "Which of the rules our class decided to follow are you now breaking?" As a subtle reminder, this would be an appropriate time for behavioral narration when you describe the behavior of cooperative students. "Henry, Louise, and Chuck have their hands raised."

Equally important as having students participate in establishing rules and procedures at the beginning of school is having students decide simultaneously what *positive and negative* consequences should result when rules are followed or ignored. Teachers frequently give attention to students who *are not* following rules and ignore students who *are* following rules and procedures and this should not be the case.

Attention to following rules can take the form of verbal or nonverbal recognition, or an actual tangible reward. Personally contacting the home through notes, phone calls, e-mails, or certificates can also serve to acknowledge a student's cooperating with following rules and procedures (Marzano, 2007). However, all of these recognitions should be placed in perspective and used intelligently.

Consequences for not following rules could include the logical consequences already described in chapter 3. One possibility may be time-out in which the student is placed in a separate area within the classroom or school itself until he or she decides to participate positively in class again. (See opposing view in Kohn, 2005).

Another possibility is overcorrection, a physical or educational act that overcompensates for misbehavior (Marzano, 2007). He describes some examples of overcorrection such as: repairing pages of all books in addition to pages a student destroyed in his own text; cleaning the entire hall after dropping food deliberately in one part; summarizing, copying, and distributing to all class members information that they were not able to learn because that student disrupted class during that time.

Regardless of whether a consequence is administered for cooperating with or not cooperating with the rules, student participation in deciding the consequences for either situation makes their imposition more effective.

Mutually determined rules and procedures should be *taught* and *practiced* in the same way that you would teach a lesson. Provide feedback to students regarding how they are performing. If necessary, reteach the rules.

As soon as the rules are decided, begin your academic lesson, and be especially sure to make it as well as all subsequent lessons *engaging*. Ratzel (2010) suggests that you do something that is simple to implement, is highly appealing to capture their interest and makes a connection between you and your students. You want to convey to your class that you mean business, will not waste time, and will do your part to make learning meaningful.

Be sure to have established procedures for events that will come up while you are teaching. It is vital that you practice, practice, practice relevant procedures. For example, when students get out of their seats, if they have the types of chairs that slide out, the students should be sure to slide the chairs back under the desk so that the aisles will be clear.

Have the students *practice* standing up, sliding the chairs under the desk, moving to an assigned location, and sitting down again several times. Eventually this procedure, as with all practiced procedures, should become a habit. You can do the same with other safety concerns such as placing bookbags/backpacks in appropriate out-of-the- way places as soon as the students enter the classroom each day.

Hunter (2004) suggested that *independence* itself be taught as a content area that should have priority over academics, especially during the beginning of school. When students learn independence, it should free up more time for the teacher to implement academic instruction. His suggestions for considering routines for independence are:

- How do we enter the classroom?
- What do we do when we first enter?
- Where are the materials needed for daily work?
- What do we do with completed work?
- What do we do with work in progress?
- What do we do when we finish an assignment?
- What is needed on the heading of a paper? (Hunter, 2004, p. 146)

What should the students do during class interruptions such as having a guest visitor, or an intercom message, or phone call? Unless you advise them otherwise, students should continue working on their assignments. However, there should be an established school procedure you must follow for emergencies such as fire drills.

What gestures should students use when they want *your* attention and what signals will you give students when you want *their* attention? To gain students' attention you can use signals already discussed previously such as but not limited to turning off or flickering the lights, ringing a bell, clapping in rhythm, raising your palm, or just standing and waiting.

What will you do with your class if a student becomes sick to his/her stomach in class? What procedures are there for leaving the room for personal or health reasons such as using the lavatory, or feeling ill?

Ordinarily, school regulations determine which procedures should be followed whenever the student is supposed to be in your class but wants to leave the room. There should be assigned times when the student can use the bathroom, pencil sharpener, wastepaper basket, library, or go to the water fountain. You will want to avoid students' drifting around or gathering in places where they can become disruptive.

How will you *distribute* materials to be used in class? There are few procedures more time-wasting than handing out papers one at a time when they could be passed back by the first person in a row or distributed by one person in a group.

How will you *collect* homework or class work efficiently? Will the students have shelves (cubbies) in which to place work folders?

How will you *return* homework or class work and where will the student keep it?

What procedures have you provided for housekeeping? You may want to set aside some time every week for routine cleaning such as washing desktops, tables, clearing out desks, or reorganizing or straightening out materials.

How will you select and rotate monitors? What functions will they serve?

What will students do when they finish work ahead of time?

How will your procedures change for students working alone, in small groups, or while other students are in groups? How much talk will you allow?

Will there be areas in your room that will be out of bounds for students unless you direct otherwise?

As important as having a procedure for entering the room is having a procedure for *exiting* the room. Communicate clearly to the students that the signal for changing classes or school dismissal is for you, not for them. After you have indicated that they may leave, will they line up, be dismissed by rows, or by groups? In order for your students not to miss the school bus, or for older students not to be late for their next class, be reasonable by keeping your eye on the clock so that you can wind up activities in sufficient time.

Establish a procedure for following directions. Be sure the directions are clear and that you have secured everyone's attention before giving directions. Tell the students that you will be giving directions and after you finish, you will call on someone to repeat them in his/her own words. Then follow through consistently.

As critical as establishing rules and procedures is regularly reviewing the effectiveness of those rules and procedures. If students constantly ignore or

**TABLE 5.1**
**Rules/Procedures Checklist**

| Rules (applicable in many different implementing circumstances) | Procedures (processes for specific routines/activities) |
|---|---|
| Working independently<br>Working in pairs<br>Working in a group (3–6)<br>Participating in whole-class instruction<br>Making up work<br>Transitions | Entering the classroom<br>Beginning the day<br>Ending the day<br>Lining up<br>Exiting the classroom<br>Handling emergencies<br>Distributing materials<br>Collecting materials<br>Cleaning up<br>Going to the restroom<br>Going to the water fountain<br>Using the pencil sharpener, waste basket<br>Requesting attention<br>Heading papers |

violate a rule or procedure, this might offer the occasion to discuss with them the specifics, remodel the steps, and have the students practice.

Sometimes a rule or procedure needs to be altered or eliminated. These occasions would occur when the rule or procedure becomes superfluous or actually interferes with the learning process. In all of these events, it is necessary to receive input from the students and discuss with them if and what changes will be necessary (Marzano, 2007).

### Self-Reflection

What process do you employ to prepare for the opening of school?

What rules/procedures have you established collaboratively (when developmentally appropriate) with your students?

What do you do to ensure that everyone follows these rules/procedures?

How do you (and the class) deal with students who do not follow rules/procedures?

Which procedures have been the most difficult to follow?

How often do you evaluate with the class the success of rules/procedures?

What rules/procedures have you eliminated or adjusted as a result of the evaluation?

# 6

# Developing Professionally

> Whoever acquires knowledge but does not practice it is as one who ploughs but does not sow.
>
> —Saadi

IN THE FIRST FIVE CHAPTERS you reviewed principles you may have already studied and have also gleaned new information. However, it is one thing to know about effective classroom management skills and another to actually be able to implement them. Knowledge of teaching skills reaches its full potential when you can translate that knowledge into performance.

## A Framework for Acquiring Teaching Skills

Learning even the most basic skills takes *time*, and developing teaching skills is a lifelong endeavor. A framework for acquiring teaching skills was offered by Joyce and Showers (1995, 2002). This framework includes: theory exploration, demonstration, practice with accompanying feedback, and adaptation and generalization.

*Theory exploration.* As a professional, the teacher must first understand the research, theory, and reasoning behind the skills or strategies to be learned or improved and the guiding principles that oversee their use. You have already accomplished this knowledge by reviewing the first five chapters and will accomplish even more when you complete part 2. You can further explore classroom management skills through additional readings and discussions with colleagues.

*Demonstration.* In this phase the skill to be improved or the new skill is modeled for the teacher. Examples of the skill in action may be conducted through a live demonstration by a peer, an outside expert, through videotapes, or computer simulations. Teachers have often complained that in their teacher education programs, there was little or no modeling of the practices professors promoted (Reiman & Thies-Sprinthall, 1998).

*Practice with accompanying feedback.* It has often been said that the three most important things in real estate are location, location, and location. It can also be said that the three most important activities in developing teaching skills are practice, practice, and practice. The role of practicing cannot be overemphasized. Practice is required to develop any skill, whether it is in the arts, sports, or teaching.

When your practice session involves *interaction with students*, as will most of the skills in this book, the practice should be recorded through audio or videotaping so that performance is documented. Documentation is of particular consequence because it has been reported *historically* that there is a gap in perception between what teachers *think* they do in the classroom and what they *actually do* (Good & Brophy, 1974; Hook and Rosenshine, 1979; Sadker & Sadker, 1994; Delpit, 1995).

Though you can practice and evaluate your own performance, *practice is more effective when it occurs with colleagues.* As soon as possible after the practice session, you should receive feedback regarding your performance from your colleagues. Immediate feedback allows you to become aware of parts of your performance that were successful, and those that needed adjustment. Receiving this feedback prevents poor performance from becoming routine.

Because your performance will be interactive in nature, microteaching—teaching a short lesson to a small group of your students, concentrating on only a few classroom management skills, usually not more than three—should be used. It is essential that the microteaching session be audio or videotaped. Since a microteaching lesson is short and focuses on just a few skills, the teacher can specifically concentrate on developing just those particular skills and evaluating them readily.

If the selected skills are those the teacher wants to acquire or increase, it is simple to count how many times they have appeared in the microteaching session. If the selected behaviors are those that should be eliminated, they also can be counted. Subsequent microteaching sessions can document the increase of effective behaviors and the decrease of those that are ineffective. Practice under microteaching conditions can then continue until the desired level of achievement has been realized.

*Adaptation and generalization.* There is no point in developing classroom management skills or any other classroom skills if they are not actually implemented in the classroom. Once the skills have been practiced in a clinical setting with a small group of your students, the skills can then be implemented with the whole class and with other small groups.

Video or audiotaping interactive skills remains a critical necessity so that you can receive feedback for yourself and from your mentors/colleagues. *In all cases it is essential that you self-evaluate and self-reflect.* Keep in mind that teacher self-reflection is one of the criteria for effective classroom management (Hanson, 1998).

## Using the Power of Coaching Rubrics

To assist you in improving your classroom management skills and in acquiring new ones, you will be provided throughout this book with a collection of personal guided observation instruments—coaching rubrics. They do exactly what their name implies by coaching and guiding your performance. A coaching rubric is a set of criteria for *developing* performance that will document your growth.

Besides serving to summarize important content throughout this book, coaching rubrics are self-reflective tools that serve many functions. Coaching rubrics expose teachers to best practices (mastery performance); offer a medium with which to internalize best practices; constantly remind teachers of best practices; analyze present teaching performance; compare present performance to best practices by identifying skills yet to be mastered; refine present skills; serve as tools for acquiring a new repertoire of skills; foster communication and dialogue among colleagues to continually identify excellent teaching criteria; provide a forum for discussing with colleagues better examples of criteria; provide a structure for adjusting criteria and for creating new rubrics when an innovation and/or new research emerges; evaluate teaching skills after practice; and document growth.

The coaching rubrics offered will empower you to take control over your own development *immediately.*

Coaching rubrics are different from scoring rubrics, which are a set of criteria for *judging* performance. In a scoring rubric the criteria (descriptors) are arranged in a hierarchy that ranges from the poorest to the best performance. A scoring rubric is holistic in that performance is either scored numerically (1–6) or verbally (such as "emerging" to "outstanding") according to a set of criteria (descriptors).

Holistic rubrics assess *overall quality* of student work such as organization of a report, creativity in writing, or critical thinking. For a score to be assigned, all criteria (descriptors) have to be taken into account *simultaneously* (Brookhart, 2004).

For example, in a scoring rubric for map legends (textbox 6.1), the following scores (1, 2, or 3) represent the corresponding performance levels.

**Textbox 6.1. Map Legend Scoring Rubric**

> Level 3 (Higher Order): Creates an original legend to communicate spatial arrangements and directions
> Level 2 (Complex): Interprets map subtleties that go beyond just reading the legend
> Level 1 (Basic): States literal meanings of legend items (Adapted from Lazear, 1998, p. 56.)

You will observe in the above scoring rubric that performance levels are ranked, and *all levels of performance have to be considered* before judging which score (1, 2, or 3) to assign.

In contrast, the criteria in coaching rubrics are *not necessarily* arranged in a hierarchy. Coaching rubrics are analytic in that each criterion (descriptor) assesses *specific aspects* of performance and is evaluated *separately* not by rating the criterion but by identifying specific and detailed examples of the criterion.

The criteria must be specific and observable enough so that more than one person observing the performance will be able to agree if each criterion had been demonstrated. Specificity and observability give the rubric reliability (Wiggins, 2005).

Coaching rubrics are easy to complete. After experience with the first coaching rubric, teachers have often expressed how simple these rubrics actually are to work with and how effective they are in improving professional practice.

As an illustration, consider The Coaching Rubric for Professional Development in table 6.2. The criteria were developed by teachers after studying

**TABLE 6.1**
**Rubrics**

| Scoring | Coaching |
|---|---|
| Judge performance | Develop performance |
| Criteria arranged in a hierarchy (performance levels) | Criteria not necessarily arranged in a hierarchy |
| All criteria evaluated together to assign a score (holistic) | Each criterion evaluated separately (analytic) |
| Score (usually numerical) assigned | Specific and accurate examples of criteria must be indicated |

## TABLE 6.2
### Coaching Rubric for Professional Development (T)

| Criteria (Descriptors) | Performance Indicators (Examples) |
|---|---|
| The teacher | |
| identified reading for personal and professional broadening | identified *Classroom Instruction That Works* by Robert Marzano et al. |
| read the materials and was able to describe what was learned | read the text, learned that the nine major instructional strategies that affect student achievement are: identifying similarities and differences; summarizing; reinforcing effort; homework and practice; using nonlinguistic representations, cooperative learning; setting objectives; generating and testing hypotheses; using questions, cues, and advance organizers. |
| used the new learning acquired from the materials in the classroom | used similarities and differences when teaching verbs by comparing them with other verbs and contrasting them with other parts of speech |
| evaluated the effect of the new learning on instruction | evaluated students on subsequent test on which they performed significantly better than they had before I made the comparisons/contrasts and just gave them definitions and examples |
| identified a relevant professional association (or associations) | identified the ASCD |
| joined the professional association(s) | joined the ASCD in June |
| participated in the association's activities and can describe what was learned | |
| transferred the new learning acquired from the professional association to the classroom and evaluated the effect of the new learning | |
| identified a mentor to assist in professional development | identified veteran master teacher Marian Floyd |
| identified others with whom to network | identified and contacted June Larson and Roy Pinzer from neighboring districts |
| collaborated with colleagues to obtain feedback for self-reflection | collaborated with fellow fourth-grade teachers Lisa, Tom, and Frank |

*(continued)*

**TABLE 6.2**
*(continued)*

| Criteria (Descriptors) | Performance Indicators (Examples) |
|---|---|
| used guided observation for self-reflection | used the Coaching Rubric for Lesson Planning and Implementation with my colleagues to evaluate my videotape |
| sought input from learners | sought input from class every Friday in both writing and in classroom discussion regarding how well the week went and what could be done to improve instruction on the part of both the students and myself |
| used a self-reflective journal | used a self-reflective journal to jot down what happened each day. Arranged with Marian Floyd to discuss my journal once a week. |
| developed a portfolio for self-reflection | |
| As a result of the above, | |
|   identified own professional development needs | |
|   devised a plan to meet the needs | |
| If learning/perfecting a particular skill/model was identified as a need for development, | |
|   explained the theory supporting the skill/model | |
| If necessary, | |
|   arranged to have the skill/model demonstrated by an expert or video simulation | |
|   practiced the skill/model with feedback (under microteaching conditions where applicable) until a desired level of achievement was attained | |
|   implemented that skill/model in the classroom with the whole class | |
|   evaluated the implementation of that skill/model in the classroom with the whole class | |

effective practices in professional development. The rubric is filled in partially to explain how to use the remaining rubrics in this book. Before you continue reading, examine this sample rubric carefully. Viewing the rubric will provide you with a frame of reference and a context for the explanation that follows.

You will notice that the coaching rubric above is divided into two columns—Criteria (Descriptors), and Performance Indicators (Examples), and that some of the Performance Indicators are completed and others are blank. The column on the left lists specific research-based skills (criteria) associated with a particular rubric. Coaching rubrics represent *mastery* performance.

When working with coaching rubrics, you should understand from the beginning that it is not expected, necessary, or in many cases possible that anyone can perform all the criteria in the rubric all the time (Wiggins, 1998). However, since the criteria are determined because they positively correlate with student achievement, implementing many of the criteria will increase the chances for reaching all learners successfully.

As already indicated, the criteria in a coaching rubric are not necessarily listed in order. For instance, you can join a professional organization before identifying reading for personal broadening. You can identify peers with whom to work before doing either of the above.

The column on the right presents the Performance Indicators. The teacher (colleagues/evaluators) must put in writing in this column *exactly how each criterion was actually demonstrated, providing specific, detailed, and appropriate examples.* This process provides objective and more reliable performance data, making it easier for several observers (peers/colleagues) to agree that the performance has actually occurred.

Documentation of the examples is more focused and precise because the same verb and tense stated in the criterion is also used in the indicator. Verbs used in the Criteria (Descriptors) are expressed in the past tense describing what the teacher actually did, *not what he or she plans to do*. For instance, the third criterion in the Coaching Rubric for Professional Development is "Enlisted peers with whom to collaborate."

*Inappropriate* ways to state the Performance Indicator would be stating what *will* be done in that category; putting a check, writing "Satisfied," "Completed," "Yes," or an equivalent term next to the corresponding criterion; numerically scoring the criterion; or offering an irrelevant example.

*Appropriate* ways of stating the Performance Indicator for the above would be writing the names of the persons who agreed to be collaborators next to the corresponding criterion, such as, "Enlisted (same verb and tense stated in the criterion) Paul and Sally from my teaching team." Otherwise, the Performance Indicator for this criterion would remain blank.

Because the documentation is so specific, coaching rubrics are more informative than the traditional type of rubric that judges performance through rating scales where raters place a check mark for each criterion in the corresponding box. Traditional rubrics, with scale variations (1–4, 1–5, 1–7), are commonly used to evaluate teachers.

However, these rubrics "don't give specific enough information . . . to use for further learning" (Brookhart, 2004, p. 77). Receiving a reported rating (score), such as 3 for Average on any scale used, while it does give some feedback, *does not inform the teacher during the self-reflective process what "Average" performance actually is or guide him or her how to improve in that category.*

You have already observed that there are blank spaces under Performance Indicators in the Coaching Rubric for Professional Development presented above. Spaces that are not filled provide specific feedback identifying where performance could be improved, unless an example demonstrated (indicator) corresponds to a negative criterion, one to be eliminated.

For example, some coaching rubrics identify negative criteria such as, "Used sarcasm in responding to a student" in the Coaching Rubric for Classroom Management that follows this section. In these cases, subsequent practice would aim at *avoiding* these negative criteria.

The first session using any rubric obtains baseline data regarding performance on that rubric. From the baseline data it can then be determined which additional criteria (descriptors) should be demonstrated or increased, and which ineffective criteria demonstrated, if any are identified as such on the rubric, should be avoided in future performance. After obtaining the baseline data, the teacher can then practice, addressing only a few criteria at one time.

In their attempt to offer a teacher evaluation system that goes beyond using observation forms and changing them periodically, Danielson & McGreal (2000) have offered a blueprint with three essential attributes: the "what," the "how," and "trained evaluators." The "what" includes clear criteria for exemplary practice based on current research; the "how" involves the ability of school districts to guarantee that teachers can demonstrate the criteria; and

**TABLE 6.3**
**Completing Performance Indicators for Corresponding Coaching Rubric Criteria**

| Correct Completion | Incorrect Completion |
|---|---|
| Use the same verb | Use a different verb |
| Use the same tense | Write what will be done |
| Provide a specific detailed example | Provide a general or vague example |
| Provide a relevant example | Provide an irrelevant example |
|  | Use terms such as "Yes," "Completed," or "Satisfied," place a check mark, or score numerically. |

"trained evaluators" who can ensure that regardless of who is conducting the evaluation, the judgment is consistent, and, therefore, reliable.

Coaching rubrics fulfill all three criteria suggested by Danielson & McGreal (2000). These rubrics express criteria for mastery performance (exemplary practice), help teachers demonstrate criteria by indicating which have and which have not been evidenced by appropriate examples thereby identifying areas needed for practice, and provide a forum for "reliable evaluations" where the teacher herself must indicate *and peer evaluators must agree* which specific and accurate examples of criteria were implemented during actual performance.

Moreover, in the discussions of the examples among all participants, suggestions can be offered for more effective examples that the teacher could have implemented. This interaction is professionalism at its best because it is highly successful in improving instruction and growth for *all* participants (Danielson, 2007).

At a time when teaching degrees, training, and certification are being questioned as definitions of a "highly qualified" teacher, a new approach has been advocated in a longitudinal study of daylong classroom observations (Pianta, 2007). "Watching teachers in action, using systematic, validated observational approaches, allows trained observers to see very clearly what good teachers do to foster learning." Coaching rubrics assist teachers and their colleague observers to ensure that agreed-upon researched criteria correlated with student achievement are understood and actually implemented in the classroom.

Using the coaching rubrics, you are now prepared to apply the framework for acquiring teaching skills (Joyce & Showers, 1995, 2002) introduced earlier in this chapter: theory exploration, demonstration, practice with feedback, and adaptation and generalization. You should understand why the criteria in the coaching rubric are essential (*theory exploration*).

Familiarity with the research and discussion with peers are crucial processes in assisting participants in both identifying and then internalizing the criteria. If there is a question about any criterion that is not clear, an example of the criterion should be provided (*demonstration*). Practicing using the coaching rubric can then follow in a controlled environment.

You may recall the old adage that practice makes perfect. Wolfe (2001) reminded teachers that practice also makes *permanent*. And Vince Lombardi taught his football players that *perfect* practice makes permanent. These are the reasons that you must practice *correctly* with complete understanding of the rubric criteria and why they are important. Frequent practice is important because not all classroom events will necessarily provide you with the occasion to demonstrate each criterion and do so consistently.

When the performance is interactive in nature within a limited time frame, microteaching should be used (*practice with accompanying feedback*). As previously stated, microteaching can be conducted with a small group of your students. If you and your colleagues are satisfied with your performance, you can then implement the new skills with your entire class (*adaptation and generalization*).

Some coaching rubrics, such as those that may be developed for lesson planning, have criteria that can be demonstrated within a class period. Other coaching rubrics take a longer time to implement, such as the Professional Development rubric offered previously and Behavior Modification (Contingency Contracting) found in part 2 of this book. Coaching rubrics that take longer than a class period to implement are coded (T).

Above all, it must be clear that coaching rubrics are *dynamic*. These living documents are *works in progress*, guidelines whose criteria should be modified when new research develops. As more studies reveal different criteria for performance excellence and as new and validated strategies and criteria are proposed, collaborators should revise rubrics and/or develop new ones.

Also, it is essential to understand that a teacher can demonstrate all the criteria in the rubric and yet be ineffective. The reason is that teaching is more than the sum of its parts. There are always intangibles involved that can contribute to effective or ineffective performance.

**Textbox 6.2.  Directions for Using Coaching Rubrics**

1. Identify collaborators (colleagues) and ensure that you and your colleagues fully understand and agree with the rubric criteria (descriptors).
2. When performance involves interacting with students, audiotape or videotape the delivery.
3. As soon as possible after the performance, document it with colleagues by writing next to each criterion under the Performance Indicators column a specific and relevant example where you demonstrated any of the criteria. Write the indicator using the same verb and same tense stated in the criterion.
4. Rubrics that take time (T) should be checked periodically to determine progress.
5. Identify no more than three additional criteria. Concentrate on only those criteria in subsequent performance using microteaching with audiotaping or videotaping whenever student interaction is involved.
6. Continue identifying additional criteria to be demonstrated in your performance and documenting that performance until a mutually agreed-upon level of achievement is reached.

## Part 1 Summary

Classroom management is multifaceted. A critical component of classroom management is arranging the environment to keep instruction flowing smoothly and keeping student misbehavior at a minimum. The demands of the twenty-first century make it necessary for students to assume more responsibility for running the classroom and for managing their own behavior.

There is a difference between discipline and punishment. Discipline is guiding the students' total development in a way that will minimize the chances for misbehavior to occur. Punishment is the imposing of a penalty for misbehavior.

Proactive measures can help avoid classroom misbehavior. Kounin offered four proactive categories to minimize classroom disruptions from occurring. These are:

1. withitness
2. group focus
3. overlapping
4. movement management

Teachers can also prevent problems by setting up a positive classroom atmosphere. This may be accomplished by having student participation in establishing rules and procedures, demonstrating sensitivity to students' feelings, identifying and capitalizing on students' strengths, and involving students in meaningful activities.

Teachers could also display a sense of humor, be constructive role models, admit mistakes, convey a positive level of expectation, offer students choices, be friendly but businesslike, and be firm yet fair. A learning environment that offers physical and emotional safety is permeated with teacher enthusiasm, provides opportunities for success, and offers student-suggested sponge activities makes it less likely that students will misbehave. Student misbehavior can also be prevented by eliminating teacher-caused problems. These include sarcasm, carrying a grudge, favoritism, making a big deal out of minor issues, being authoritarian as opposed to authoritative, ignoring students' strengths, assigning busy work, and implementing rules and procedures inconsistently.

Once disruptions occur, there are reactive measures that teachers can take. It is important that these measures are educative and keep the flow of instruction. Among these measures are: using silence, gestures, and peers to correct misbehavior; emphasizing the positive; expressing your feelings; asking a student to write or state the misbehavior; moving to the area near the disruption; accentuating the positive; and applying logical consequences.

Punishment can be contrived or naturally occurring (result as a logical consequence). Whenever possible, teachers should use logical consequences in correcting misbehavior.

Students' academic and emotional needs should be the first consideration in setting up the classroom. Physical features of the room and safety factors must also be taken into account.

The first days of school set a tone for the rest of the year. Begin by establishing rules and procedures with input from the class. These rules and procedures should be few, brief, and stated in positive terms and should cover ways to enter and exit the room, distribute and return materials, make up work, keep the room neat, and participate appropriately in classroom instruction.

At the time rules and procedures are established, both positive and negative consequences for following them should also be determined. Then rules and procedures should be formally taught and practiced and implemented consistently.

Effective classroom management skills as well as all other teaching skills can be obtained by understanding the theory behind them, having the skills demonstrated, practicing the skills with feedback, and transferring them to the classroom. As with all other skills, teaching skills take time and practice to develop.

Coaching rubrics are guided observation instruments that assist teachers in acquiring, developing, and evaluating, teaching skills.

The coaching rubric in table 6.4 was developed by teachers after studying the first five chapters in this book. Use this coaching rubric to analyze and improve your classroom management skills.

**TABLE 6.4**
**Coaching Rubric for Classroom Management (T)**

*Proactive Phase: Effective Classroom Management Practices to Prevent Problems*

| Criteria (Descriptors) | Performance Indicators (Examples) |
|---|---|
| The teacher . . .<br>implemented an engaging instructional system with a variety of approaches and assessments<br>conveyed and implemented expectation that all would support each other to succeed<br>established with input from students (when age appropriate) no more than eight brief, clear rules stated in positive terms<br>secured student input regarding consequences for both following and not following rules<br>established with input from students (when age appropriate) procedures to make the class run smoothly. | |

| Criteria (Descriptors) | Performance Indicators (Examples) |
|---|---|
| practiced rules/procedures with class<br>implemented rules/procedures consistently<br>called each student by name<br>evidenced awareness of what each student was doing all the time<br>managed transitions from one activity to another smoothly<br>demonstrated respect for each student<br>worked unpopular students into groups and lessons<br>interacted with students in a friendly but businesslike manner<br>used "You" messages to reinforce positive work and behavior<br>reflected to identify any teacher-caused student misbehavior problems<br>established with class input *improved* procedures/routines/classroom setup, etc. as a result of analyzing less efficient past practices | |

*Reactive Phase: Effective Classroom Management Practices to Handle Problems* Once They Have Occurred

| Criteria (Descriptors) | Performance Indicators (Examples) |
|---|---|
| The teacher . . .<br>  remained calm<br>waited for attention<br>involved the class first in solving the problem, when appropriate<br>used nonverbal signals<br>moved immediately to area of disruption<br>used any misbehaving student's name in context<br>used behavioral narration<br>removed any interfering physical object(s) casually without breaking the flow of instruction<br>reassigned seating to misbehaving student(s)<br>recognized behavior opposite the misbehavior<br>used "I" messages<br>applied naturally occurring (logical) consequences<br>addressed misbehaving student(s) personally and privately<br>requested that a misbehaving student state or write the misbehavior | |

*(continued)*

**TABLE 6.4**
*(coninued)*

*Ineffective Classroom Management Practices (Those to Be Eliminated)*

| Criteria (Descriptors) | Performance Imdicators (Examples) |
|---|---|
| The teacher . . .<br>used authoritarian methods to control the class<br>spoke over students' voices<br>exhibited favoritism<br>demonstrated resentment toward student(s)<br>made a sarcastic or other inappropriate remark(s)<br>assigned busy work<br>implemented rules and routines inconsistently | |

# II

# REVIEWING/ACQUIRING CLASSROOM MANAGEMENT STRATEGIES (SYSTEMS)

# 7

# The Necessity for Reviewing/Acquiring Specific Classroom Management Strategies

IN THE PREVIOUS CHAPTERS you reexamined research-based guidelines for preventing and dealing with classroom management problems, especially as they relate to twenty-first-century classrooms. As you develop skill in implementing these guidelines, you should review and expand your repertoire to include specific student-centered through teacher-centered strategies (models, systems) for dealing with different types of students and behavior problems.

Studying this range of strategies will help you put into perspective the recommendations in the previous chapters so that you can deepen your professional understanding regarding not only what works, but also *why* it should work.

You also read that classroom management theory is based on learning theory. The major learning theories are behavioral, cognitive, and constructivist. "Even though theorists argue which model is the best, most excellent teachers apply all . . . approaches as appropriate" (Woolfolk, 2004, p. 313). Woolfolk goes on to say that instead of debating the virtues of each approach,

> consider their contributions to understanding learning and improving teaching. Don't feel that you must choose the "best" approach—there is no such thing. . . . Different views of learning can be used together to create productive learning environments *for the diverse students you will teach* (emphasis mine). Behavioral theory helps us understand the role of cues in setting the stage for behaviors and the role of consequences and practice in encouraging or discouraging behaviors. But much of humans' lives and learning is more than behaviors. Language and higher-order thinking require complex information

processing and memory—something the cognitive models of the thinker-as-computer have helped us understand. And what about the person as a creator and constructor of knowledge, not just a processor of information? Here, constructivist perspectives have much to offer.

I like to think of the three main learning theories . . . as pillars for teaching. Students must first understand and make sense of the material (constructivist); then they must remember what they have understood (cognitive-information processing); and then they must practice and apply (behavioral) their new skills and understanding to make them more fluid and automatic—a permanent part of their repertoires. Failure to attend to any part of the process means lower-quality learning (Woolfolk, 2008, pp. 398–99).

Churchward (2009) raises the point that experts in the field of discipline often disagree. He cites as an example, the student-centered Teacher Effectiveness Training approach of Thomas Gordon (1974) with the more teacher-centered Assertiveness Training approach of Lee Canter (1992, 2001).

Assuming that both of them are correct, Churchward (2009) suggests that *they may not be talking about the same students.* He believes that just as we would not teach all students the same way in different subject areas, we should not set up the same discipline systems that treat all students the same.

Based on the stages of moral development offered by Kohlberg (1981), Churchward proposes four stages of discipline:

Stage 1: The power (recalcitrant behavior) stage in which might makes right. Students at this stage require a lot of attention and are frequently defiant, refusing to follow directions. By age four or five students usually progress beyond this stage. However, some older students may still function at this level.

Stage 2: The reward/punishment (self-serving behavior) stage. In this "what's in it for me" stage, students behave because there is a reward that they can receive, such as candy, a sticker, or free time, or behave properly because they do not like what may happen to them if they don't behave (scolding, withholding a reward, isolation). By eight or nine years of age most students tend to move beyond this stage.

Stage 3: Interpersonal discipline (mutual interpersonal) stage. At this level students are concerned with "how can I please you?" They behave because they are asked to, want to be liked, and care what others think of them. This stage is representative of most students in middle/junior high school.

Stage 4: Social order (self-discipline) stage. Students who reach this level have a sense of right and wrong. They can be left alone and still complete tasks. Many middle/junior high school students function at this level occasionally, however, few do so consistently. Although most students do not usually function at this stage, they are close enough to it to understand it.

All people work their way through these stages of moral development (stages of discipline). When you can identify the stage in which the student is functioning, you can then help that student move on to the next level.

Churchward (2009) believes that it is a mistake to attempt to force a student to skip stages. Demanding that a Stage 1 student behave like a Stage 4 student is not a reasonable expectation and will, therefore, lead to frustration. Helping students work through the four stages is all the more reason that the teacher should possess and use many different strategies.

Currently, some strategies based on behavior theory may be out of favor. However, even these strategies can be adjusted to include several contemporary classroom management attributes. When these opportunities occur, they will be emphasized.

In a major study on classroom management, the Classroom Strategy Study conducted by Brophy (1996), the conclusion of the research was that not only did effective teachers have a set of different classroom management skills and strategies, but these teachers also used *different* strategies matched to the needs of different types of students.

Yet, it has been debated among classroom management experts whether or not teachers should use an eclectic approach when applying these systems or stay with a single system (cf. Wolfgang [1999] with Tauber [1999, 2007]). After you have read part 2, you may be on your way to deciding this question for yourself.

A strategy, also known as a system or model, has two basic parts—theory and practice. The theory describes the concepts and principles that explain why the strategy should work. Theory, however, reaches its full potential only when it can be put into practice in the classroom. After you understand the theory, you will learn *how* to apply it using the coaching rubric for that strategy. The amount of practice with the rubric will determine eventually *how well* you learned the strategy.

As you go through each strategy, you should be asking yourself the following questions: *For whom* would the strategy be most appropriate? *What* behaviors could best be developed with this strategy? And under what conditions, or *when* would the strategy be best applied? Also consider how contemporary classroom management practices would be reflected in each strategy, and if not, how it could be adjusted to include desired twenty-first-century classroom characteristics.

It is important to understand that any strategy you implement with your class should not conflict with your philosophy of discipline or your personality.

Attempting to do so would lead to a halfhearted approach, one without conviction, and it would be perceived as such by the students.

Before you continue reading this chapter, it may be helpful for you to have a philosophy/personality check. Answer yes, no, or sometimes to the following.

Do you believe that . . .

> you know what is best for your students?
> in a disagreement with a student, one of you should win?
> students should be praised (rewarded)?
> you should control the environment?
> you should impose discipline procedures?
> your students have free will?
> you should encourage students?
> students have the innate ability to solve their own problems?
> your function is that of a facilitator?
> you are assertive?
> you are easy-going (laissez-faire)?

When you complete this part, you will go back to these beliefs to see if the strategies you favor support your beliefs. As you study each strategy, keep in mind the following continuum:

Gordon→→Dreikurs→→Glasser→→Canter & Canter→→Skinner

At one end of this continuum is the humanist approach (Gordon); at the other end is the behaviorist approach (Skinner).

| Humanist | Behaviorist |
|---|---|
| Student-centered | Teacher-centered |
| Student power | Teacher power |
| Noninterventionist | Interventionist |
| Facilitating | Directing |
| Nurturing | Controlling |

Wolfgang (2005) describes the humanist-through-behaviorist approaches as a power continuum of basic discipline philosophies reflecting the action a teacher could take, from the minimum to the maximum. He further identified these actions in the same order (minimum to maximum) as: Relationship-Listening; Confronting-Contracting; and Rules and Consequences.

# 8
# Teacher Effectiveness Training (T.E.T.)

## Theory

THOMAS GORDON PROPOSED HIS SAME THEORY with different environmental applications in three books: *P.E.T.: Parent Effectiveness Training* (1970); *T.E.T.: Teacher Effectiveness Training* (1974); and *L.E.T.: Leader Effectiveness Training* (1977). Gordon was greatly influenced by Carl Rogers (1969, 1971, 1981), a psychologist and therapist who believed that there is an inner rational person in all human beings. This inner rational person gives the human being the innate ability to solve his or her own problems. Self-actualization, the realization of one's personal potential, is the driving force in human behavior. According to this belief, it is the role of the teacher to assist the student in becoming self-actualized.

Rogers promoted the idea that the key to developing subject matter in school is through human relations concepts. Therefore, the teacher is more a counselor than a teacher. The teacher is a nurturer or facilitator who through supportive, open, and honest communication with students creates a learning environment that fosters personal, social, and academic growth.

At the core of Gordon's T.E.T. is open and authentic communication between teacher and student. In order to be effective, communication, with its prefix co-, meaning "with" or "together," must go *two ways*. The teacher understands the student *and* the student understands the teacher. They continue to respond to each other in ways that deepen understanding.

Teachers must learn to decipher the student's real message and feelings when he speaks or behaves in a certain way. In attempting to interpret what the student is communicating, the teacher should use the least amount of control possible. If the teacher solves a problem for a student that he can solve for himself, the teacher is not helping the student.

Using a T.E.T. model, the teacher first looks at a student who is misbehaving in a way that says, "I know what you are doing, I trust your capability to come up with your own solution to your misbehavior, and I am here to help you find that solution." If a student cannot solve the problem immediately, the teacher encourages (not forces) the student to verbalize the problem. During this encouragement period, the teacher provides time for the student to think about the problem, carefully avoiding judgmental verbal or nonverbal communication.

Gordon believes that open communication is often blocked by directive statements that teachers use, thus cutting off the very communication the teacher is trying to attain. These "roadblocks" include, among others: commanding, threatening, warning, preaching, offering logical arguments, consoling, criticizing, agreeing, ridiculing, diagnosing, praising, interrogating, and humoring. All of these roadblocks, according to Gordon, even those that on the surface seem positive, prevent the student from coming up with his or her own solution.

## Implementation

In order to implement the T.E.T. strategy for solving a problem, the teacher must first determine who owns the problem; depending on ownership, the method of dealing with the problem will be different. There are three ownership choices: the student, the teacher, or both.

If the student owns the problem, she or he will be the only one affected by it.

### Examples of Student Problem Ownership
She wasn't selected to be in the marching band.
Other students pick on him on the school bus.
Someone keeps taking her lunch, money, pens, or other possessions.

When handling a student-owned problem, Gordon suggests that the teacher use the following: critical listening, door openers, or active listening.

- Critical listening. The teacher can remain silent, communicating acknowledgment-type listening through eye contact, gestures, and posture.

Noncommittal remarks such as "Uh-huh," "I see," and "Oh, gee," can also tell the student that the teacher is listening and particularly aware of the student's feelings.
- Door openers. If the student seems willing, the teacher communicates the readiness to listen to the student's problem. "Do you want to discuss it?" and "Tell me more" are the types of statements that advise the student that when he is ready, right then or in the future, the teacher is available to listen.
- Active listening. The teacher reflects the message and feelings associated with it by paraphrasing what the student says. "What you are telling me is that you feel disappointed that you didn't do as well as you expected on the test" is a reflective statement made by a teacher to a student's frustrated statement such as, "I thought I should've gotten at least an 80 on that exam."

Note how different critical listening, door openers, and active listening are from the previously mentioned "roadblocks" teachers tend to use.

If the teacher owns the problem, it is one that tangibly and concretely affects him or her.

### Examples of Teacher Problem Ownership

A student constantly calls out, interrupting the teacher's train of thought.

A student mixes up materials, making it difficult for the teacher to distribute them in a timely way.

In both examples the student is essentially unaffected by the misbehavior.

When dealing with teacher-owned problems, Gordon recommends that the teacher send the misbehaving student an "I" message. You were already introduced to different types of "I" messages in chapter 3. As a reminder, Gordon's "I" message has three component parts:

1. The student's misbehavior
2. How the misbehavior concretely and tangibly affects the teacher
3. How the misbehavior makes the teacher feel

### Examples

"When you constantly call out the answers (statement of the student's misbehavior), it interrupts my train of thought (description of how the misbehavior concretely affects the teacher), and *I* feel frustrated" (description of how the misbehavior makes the teacher feel.

**TABLE 8.1**
Coaching Rubric for Teacher Effectiveness Training
(T [time] depends on who owns the problem)

| Criteria (Descriptors) | Performance Indicators (Examples) |
|---|---|
| The teacher . . . determined who owned the problem—the teacher, the student, or both. | |
| If the STUDENT owned the problem, the teacher encouraged (not forced) the student to put the problem in his or her own words<br>listened critically during the student's verbalizing<br>used door openers<br>listened actively. | |
| If the TEACHER owned the problem, the teacher sent an "I" message that . . .<br>stated WHAT the student was doing or has done to affect the teacher<br>indicated HOW that student's behavior tangibly affected the teacher<br>expressed how that behavior made the teacher FEEL. | |
| If BOTH THE TEACHER AND THE STUDENT owned the problem, the teacher . . .<br>implemented the "no lose" method<br>defined the problem<br>generated with student possible problem solutions<br>encouraged solutions from student without evaluating them at this point. | |
| When enough solutions were generated, the teacher . . .<br>evaluated with student each solution individually<br>made a decision with student regarding which solution(s) to employ<br>implemented the solution(s)<br>evaluated the implemented solution(s). | |
| If necessary, the teacher . . .<br>repeated the "no lose" method. | |

"If you constantly mix up these materials (statement of the misbehavior), it makes it difficult for me to sort out what my students need (description of how the misbehavior concretely affects the teacher), and *I* feel angry (description of teacher's feeling).

Gordon believes that teachers often hide their feelings, and that it is important to communicate with students on the feelings level. Students often are unaware how their behavior affects the teacher's feelings, and once the students are alerted, they tend to act in a way that avoids upsetting the teacher. Besides, as shared leaders in classroom management, it is legitimate for teachers as well as for students to also show their feelings.

When *both* the student and teacher own the problem, Gordon offers the "no lose" method for problem resolution, where both the teacher and student win. An example of a problem owned by both student and teacher is the following: The student is constantly misplacing her pens and becomes frustrated. When she needs a pen, she removes it from the teacher's desk. When the teacher needs a pen, he is constantly fishing for one.

The "no lose" method, a variation of the scientific method, has six steps.

1. Problem definition. The teacher employs active listening and "I" messages to focus on a problem for the purpose of communicating his needs and having the student communicate her needs.
2. Tentative solution generation. The teacher encourages the student to brainstorm in order to come up with as many possible solutions to resolving the problem. The teacher should be careful not to evaluate any solutions offered at this point, just to record them.
3. Solution evaluation. The teacher and student evaluate which tentative solutions will meet both their needs.
4. Solution selection. Based on the solution evaluation, teacher and student arrive at a consensus regarding which solution has the best chance for success in meeting both their needs.
5. Solution implementation. Teacher and student decide how to put the solution into effect and when to begin.
6. Solution evaluation. Periodically, both parties meet to decide how well the solution is working; whether or not it needs modifications; and, if necessary, whether both should begin the entire process again to come up with a new solution.

# 9

# Social Discipline

## Theory

SOCIAL DISCIPLINE WAS DEVELOPED BY RUDOLPH DREIKURS (1968). He was influenced by the work of the social psychologist Alfred Adler from the Freudian school of psychology. Adler believed that the need to belong and be accepted by others was the core motivation of all humans.

All behavior, both positive and misbehavior, is purposeful, orderly, and aimed toward achieving social recognition. It is the "inner" goals that result in "outward" behavior. Therefore, it is the teacher's role to assist students who misbehave to recognize their "inner" goals and guide these students to develop the more appropriate goal of learning how to belong with others.

Students want recognition and evidence that they matter. Students who are unsuccessful in obtaining this social recognition develop a pattern of misbehavior. They try to fulfill "inner" needs by behavior that is annoying, hostile, helpless, or destructive. Dreikurs believed that teachers should help students understand their faulty (mistaken) goals and give students the means for group acceptance. Then these students will rationally change their own behavior.

There are subconscious goals that motivate misbehavior. Dreikurs identifies them as:

1. Attention seeking. This behavior is demonstrated by a student who is constantly looking to belong and be recognized. The student feels as though he is part of the class only when he gets attention from the

teacher or from other class members. However, instead of seeking this recognition through productive work, the student may behave in ways that demand constant praise or criticism. Some examples of attention-seeking behaviors include being a wise guy, class jester and show-off; getting "in your face"; and causing a general nuisance.

2. Power and Control. This goal is demonstrated by a student who feels inferior, unable to meet her own expectations or those of others. Whether the student is actually handicapped or has a false perception of inferiority does not matter. In either situation the student will attempt to remediate the perception by attempting to be argumentative; defiant; deliberately disobedient; rebellious; or by exhibiting temper tantrums.
3. Revenge. When a student cannot gain the first two goals, attention and power, he then develops the goal of revenge. The student perceives himself as having unequal status as a result of what others have done to him. He feels hurt by others and this feeling gives him the "right" to make others hurt. The student opts to achieve status not through attention or control but through humiliation of others and through malicious or violent acts against others.
4. Helplessness/Inadequacy. At this stage the student gives up on achieving group status or even group membership. She feels unfairly treated, uncared for, and not equal to other class members. What is most problematic is that the student feels that she has no ability (positive or destructive) to do anything about it. She accepts being an outsider and does not care.

## Implementation

The teacher must determine which of the above goals the student is seeking. This goal identification can be accomplished by the teacher's answers to three (internal) questions.

### Question One: How does the student's misbehavior make you feel?

When students are constantly exhibiting attention-seeking behaviors, teachers will generally feel *annoyed* and wish the student would just disappear. When students demonstrate power-and-control goals, teachers believe that their authority has been challenged and they feel *angry* or *intimidated*. Students who have the goal of revenge make the teacher feel *hurt*. Lastly, when the student exhibits the goal of helplessness/inadequacy, teachers feel *incapable* or a sense of *despair*.

After guessing which goal the student is exhibiting, the teacher makes a directive statement followed by a logical consequence (chapter 3).

> Example: Charles has spray-painted the lockers of several students. (Revenge)
> The teacher says, "Charles, before you can go to lunch, you have to remove the paint from the lockers.

Once the teacher suspects from her own reaction (annoyed, angry, hurt, or intimidated) a student's faulty goals, the teacher can verify whether or not her guess was correct. This can be accomplished by asking the student if he wishes to know why he behaves the way he does. If the student shows interest, the teacher then asks four sequential questions (overt) while simultaneously determining verification through a "recognition reflex" exhibited by the student's body language or verbal behavior. These questions are:

1. (Attention goal) Is it possible that you want special attention?
2. (Power goal) Is it that you hope to get your own way and want to be boss?
3. (Revenge goal) Is it that you want to hurt others just as you feel they have hurt you?
4. (Helplessness goal) Is it just that you want to be left alone?

Verification can be obtained when in response to any one question the student chuckles, smiles, jerks his head, laughs, moves shoulders, or shows other behaviors that respond to the goal implied in the question.

Once the teacher believes that she has diagnosed the faulty student goal, treatment can then be implemented.

## Question Two: How have you responded consistently to the student's misbehavior?

It is usual practice for teachers to actually reward students for attention-seeking behaviors. Teachers may call on students who call out, or constantly remind them not to do it, thereby reinforcing attention-seeking behaviors. Students who exhibit power goals can frequently cause teachers to get involved in a power struggle in which the student constantly tests the teacher.

Students respond to revenge goals by trying to get even with other students. Because teachers find this behavior distasteful, they find it difficult to warm up to revenge-seeking students and may tend to ignore them, though warmth and caring is just what these students need. Students seeking inadequacy goals may lead the teacher to just give up. These teacher responses exacerbate the situation with the students in question.

**Question Three: How has the student responded to your way of dealing with remediation?**

While examining responses to the third question, teachers find that students become less independent and responsible when attention-seeking behaviors are reinforced by constantly coaxing and reminding students to behave properly. If the teacher fights back with power-seeking students, the power struggle escalates. Students who appear to comply do so defiantly.

When a teacher retaliates against a revenge-seeking student, the student could become hostile and/or violent and exhibit more vengeful behavior. Finally, teachers who give up on helpless/inadequate students reinforce the mistaken belief that they are incapable.

Dreikurs believed that in dealing with students, natural and logical consequences and encouragement should be used. He did not believe in positive or negative reinforcement, or in praise or punishment.

In a natural consequence, that which occurs as a result of a behavior occurs by itself. For example, a child who runs to recess instead of walking in line falls and gets hurt. In a logical consequence, the result of a behavior is imposed but directly related to the behavior. For example, a student who steals a pen must replace it.

Dreikurs also distinguished between praise, which he believed should be avoided, and encouragement, which he thought should be fostered. When using praise, the teacher draws attention to being pleased by the student and to the student's accomplishing a complete product. When using encouragement, the teacher fosters an atmosphere of optimism and respect.

This atmosphere is accomplished by avoiding competition situations for the student; placing her in a group that is willing to help; emphasizing progress instead of a perfect product; and passing judgment on the student's misbehaviors, not on the student herself.

The difference between praise and encouragement can be illustrated by comparing the "You" and "I" messages already presented in table 2.1 (chapter 2) and reproduced as table 9.1. "You" messages are those that foster encouragement; "I" messages are those that give praise.

**TABLE 9.1
Comparing "You" and "I" Messages**

| "You" Messages (Encouragement) | "I" Messages (General) (Praise) |
|---|---|
| You did a great job helping Larry learn his multiplication facts. | I think you did a great job helping Larry with multiplication. |
| You worked so hard on your composition that you raised your score 10 points. | I'm proud that you raised your score 10 points. |
| You cleaned up so well after lab that the other students imitated you. | I liked the way you cleaned up your lab table. |

**TABLE 9.2**
**Summary of the Dreikurs Theory**

| Faulty Goals | Corresponding Behaviors | Teacher Feelings | Usual Teacher Responses | Appropriate Responses |
|---|---|---|---|---|
| Attention | Persistently acts to gain attention even when asked to stop | Annoyed | Provides attention to student | Ignore attention-getting behavior, reward opposite behavior, move near student |
| Power/Control | When asked to stop attention-seeking behaviors, becomes defiant, accelerates negative behavior, and confronts teacher | Intimidated/Beaten | Gets involved in battle for power | Avoid power struggle, deal with student without class present |
| Revenge | Hurts others mentally or physically | Hurt/Wronged | Avoids a caring relationship with student | Establish logical consequences, elicit student's response to consequences |
| Helplessness | Avoids social contact with others, is passive, avoids academic work | Incapable | Gives up | Create opportunities for success, recognize improvement, connect mistakes with growth opportunities |

When dealing with attention-seeking students, the teacher should devise ways to let those students receive legitimate attention. This may be accomplished by setting aside a specific time when the student can share with his peers some work he has done, or a story/joke he would like to tell. When the student is behaving properly, the teacher can go over to him and speak to him personally. In working with power-seeking students, the teacher can give them power through legitimate means such as leading the line, collecting lunch money, or being the playground monitor.

**TABLE 9.3**
**Coaching Rubric for Social Discipline (T)**

| Criteria (Descriptors) | Performance Indicators (Examples) |
|---|---|
| The teacher . . .<br>gathered data on student (the way she behaves with classmates, other teachers, family members, other people)<br>reflected on his own feelings involving the student (annoyed, beaten, hurt, helpless)<br>responded with a relevant directive statement that included a logical consequence<br>confronted the student at a calmer time as to whether or not she wanted to know why she behaves the way she does. | |
| If the student was receptive, the teacher . . .<br>asked the four sequential questions (overt) that relate to the faulty goals of attention, power, revenge, and helplessness. (Is it possible that you are looking for attention? Could it be that you want to be boss? Is it that you want to hurt others? Do you want to be left alone?) | |
| Immediately after each question, the teacher . . .<br>determined whether the student exhibited a "recognition reflex" verifying her goal. | |
| After conferring with the student, the teacher . . .<br>established through directive statements a long-range plan describing how the student can meet her needs through socially appropriate behavior<br>enlisted the class as a model of democratic living by having members offer ways to help the student<br>used natural/logical consequences for inappropriate behaviors that may persist while simultaneously using encouragement. | |

Avoid confronting a student who refuses to do work by telling her casually that she can decide in an hour when it will be completed. *Then follow through.* Students who are revenge-seeking must be handled in a caring manner, which may be opposite to the way the teacher actually feels. Tell the student that she is cared for and ask her how to improve the class. Share a special time with the student with private chats and be sure to say a cheerful "Hi" to the student each day.

You may want to reflect upon whether the student who demonstrates faulty goals would still be demonstrating them if the teacher had set up a supportive classroom environment at the beginning of school and had reinforced this environment consistently. Students who are shared leaders in a caring classroom community are responsible for the success of all class members. As such, these students, in addition to the teacher, should be able to assist the student in eliminating faulty goals and in replacing them with more productive goals.

# 10

# Reality Therapy

## Theory

WILLIAM GLASSER, INITIALLY TRAINED in Freudian psychoanalysis, came up with his own classroom management theory dealing with behavior problems, which he described in several books (*Schools without Failure*, 1969; *Reality Therapy: A New Approach to Psychiatry*, 1975; *Control Theory in the Classroom*, 1986; and *The Quality School: Managing Students without Coercion*, 1992).

Glasser found that in working with his patients, dwelling on the past, a common practice in Freudian psychoanalysis, was inefficient. Students must live in the present, the here and now, which is *reality* for them. The present is where they make choices. In the real world these choices must satisfy the student's needs without depriving others of their needs.

Glasser rejects working with the unconscious or having teachers being nonjudgmental and accepting of misbehavior. He believes that students are responsible for their own behavior, must accept the consequences of that behavior, and must commit themselves to act in a way that is responsible toward others. It is the teacher's role to structure an environment—reality therapy—that will assist students in making responsible choices.

## Implementation

A reality therapy environment has certain attributes:

- Student involvement. Reality therapy is contemporary in its approach because the school itself is perceived by the student as a positive place where warm and caring teachers help students become involved in improving their own behavior as well as their learning.
- Misbehavior identification. Once involvement is secured, the teacher has the student identify his own misbehavior, thus *avoiding taking away responsibility for the misbehavior*. When the student misbehaves, the teacher keeps him focused on the present by asking, "*What* are you doing?" It is important to focus on the "what" because students are often unaware of exactly what they are doing.
- If the student can bring this to consciousness, it is a valuable first step in getting him to correct the misbehavior. The teacher must be persistent in insisting on the student's verbalizing the "what" because the student will often state what someone else did or "why" he misbehaved, which gives an excuse, not responsibility, for the misbehavior.
- Cause and effect. The teacher has the student state the relationship between the misbehavior and its result. A student who throws objects around the room (the cause) could have as a result the injuring of another student (the effect). Practicing having students state what effects their misbehavior can have will eventually help the students internalize the results of their misbehavior and the necessity for changing it.
- Devising a plan. Once the student has identified the misbehavior and its results, the *onus is on her to devise a plan to correct the misbehavior*. Choosing her own plan is effective in taking responsibility for implementing it and taking charge of her life. If the student is surprised or confused by being asked to create a plan and cannot offer suggestions, the teacher gives the student time to come up with a plan that is mutually acceptable.

    The teacher should not get caught up in the trap of constructing a plan for the student. This is particularly important for the contemporary classroom manager, who is a coach and facilitator and wants to encourage student self-regulation.
- Securing a *commitment*. Have the student sign a contract or make some other kind of formal agreement that he will implement the plan and that the teacher will be available to assist the student in carrying it out. This is an example of shared responsibility in twenty-first-century classroom management.

- Accepting no excuses. If the plan is not working, take a fresh look at it, revise it, or come up with a new plan. There is no room for excuses, for they deal with the past, not the present (reality), or future.
- Applying logical consequences. Glasser believes that if the student does not implement the plan, *logical consequences* should be imposed by the teacher. You already read about logical consequences in chapter 3. Logical consequences are rational results that follow—identifiable, reasonable connections between the misbehavior and the consequences. If a student does not study, she will not do as well as she could or could possibly fail. If the student is hurling an object across the room, the object is taken away. Logical consequences are different from punishment, which takes responsibility away from the student and frequently has little to do with the misbehavior. Punishment also negates the feeling of the first attribute listed above, that school is a warm and caring place.
- Being persistent. It is made clear to the student and to the rest of the class that the teacher will be *consistent, insistent,* and persistent in demanding that the above be carried out.

## The Classroom Meeting

One of the most important applications of Reality Therapy is the Classroom Meeting. The underlying theory for both is the same. In the Classroom Meeting the teacher structures regular time and procedures for handling problems that come up in class. *Both the teacher and the class share responsibility for solving any problems,* an important attribute of the contemporary classroom. The success of this model in a twenty-first-century classroom also assumes that a caring classroom environment has been established.

Problems for discussion may be related to the curriculum, the classroom organization, an individual, or to class misbehavior problems. To use the Classroom Meeting for an individual problem, it should be the type of problem that goes beyond the teacher and student and *affects the entire class.* An example would be with bullying behavior.

The students sit in a circle and the teacher conveys the message that everyone, including the teacher, is free to state feelings, opinions, or offer suggestions. There are no right or wrong answers. Students must speak to each other with civility and, consistent with the principles of reality therapy, concentrate on what may be done in the present and future, not what happened in the past. As in Teacher Effectiveness Training, the teacher encourages participation by critical listening and using gestures and nondirective comments, without forcing anyone to speak.

**TABLE 10.1**
**Coaching Rubric for Reality Therapy (T)**

| Criteria (Descriptors) | Performance Indicators (Examples) |
|---|---|
| Before implementing the strategy, the teacher . . . reflected seriously on past behavior with the student | |
| If the past behavior was negative, the teacher . . . identified a new method of dealing with the student expected that this method would be successful. | |
| After considering the above, the teacher . . . established a caring and warm relationship with the misbehaving student defined clear boundaries of acceptable behavior. | |
| If misbehavior then occurred, the teacher . . . confronted the student and told him or her to stop the unacceptable behavior avoided warnings and insults while performing the above kept the student focused on the irresponsible behavior. | |
| If the previous procedures did not work, the teacher . . . posed questions to make the misbehaving student think rationally about the misbehavior by asking, "What are you doing?" while carefully avoiding "why" questions posed the question, "How does (whatever the behavior the student stated) help you?" posed the question, "What are you going to do about your behavior?" | |
| If there was no respond to what the question of what the student was going to do about the behavior, the teacher . . . had the student commit to designing a contract as either a signed plan of his or her own (the preferable method) or one co-designed with the teacher. | |
| If the student violated the plan, the teacher . . . enforced the logical consequences of privilege loss. | |
| If the student failed to carry out the plan, the teacher . . . imposed class isolation where the student was confronted and told to stop the behavior asked again "what" questions pressured to come up with a new plan and commitment confronted with mutually agreed-upon logical consequences. | |

Glasser (1975, 1992) suggested three different types of classroom meetings: open-ended, educational/diagnostic, and problem-solving.

Open-ended meetings may be used to explore ideas presented by students, or discuss imaginary problems. "What would we do if schools were permanently closed but we would have to be educated?" is an example of an imaginary, open-ended problem for exploration.

The educational/diagnostic meeting could be used to help the teacher make curricular and/or instructional decisions. What do students already know about a unit to be taught? What would they like to learn? What activities would they like to be involved with so they could learn effectively? How is a unit proceeding so far, and what changes could be made to improve achievement?

In the problem-solving meeting, the class concentrates on a problem that affects all students. They identify the problem, gather data, generate solutions, and design a plan for the problem's solution. "What should be done about stealing in the class?" and, "How can we improve civility in the classroom?" are examples of general problems for classroom meeting discussions.

A critical use of the classroom meeting is dealing with a specific problem of one particular student. A student who bullies others, makes up lies about them, or physically attacks others would be the subject of such a meeting. Glasser believes that when a student's behavior affects the entire class, that student should be confronted and assisted by the entire class. The purpose of the meeting should be making the student cognizant of his/her misbehavior and accept responsibility for its consequences.

Even though there is shared responsibility in the contemporary classroom, the teacher must maintain *firm control* over this type of meeting so that it does not burgeon into fighting or yelling. The teacher should explain and enforce that everyone should treat each other with respect while they all discuss the student's misbehavior, and that the purpose of the meeting is to help the offending student behave in a more appropriate manner.

The teacher then asks each student in the class in a nonconfrontational way to:

a. face individually the misbehaving student;
b. state exactly what the offense was; and
c. describe how the offense affected him or her personally and/or physically.

The teacher then does the same.

When everyone has completed the description of the misbehavior and its effects, the misbehaving student is given the chance to give his side of the story and explain what other students in the class may have done to him.

**TABLE 10.2**
**Coaching Rubric for the Classroom Meeting**

| Criteria (Descriptors) | Performance Indicators (Examples) |
|---|---|
| The teacher . . . explained the purpose of the meeting (educational/diagnostic, problem-solving, open-ended) arranged seating so that all students faced each other emphasized that in the meeting every student should feel free to express ideas, feelings, and opinions indicated that there were no wrong answers kept emphasis on the present encouraged all to participate without forcing. | |
| If the meeting involved a student whose misbehavior affected many students, the teacher . . . conducted a problem-solving meeting where the entire class confronted the misbehaving student explained the reason for the meeting kept strong control over the meeting to avoid improper language and name calling conducted the meeting, reinforcing the purpose of problem solution asked every student one at a time to face the misbehaving student and state what the misbehavior was asked every student to describe how the misbehavior personally affected each student physically and/or emotionally. | |
| When all had the opportunity to speak, the teacher . . . asked the misbehaving student to explain what others in the class had done to interfere with him or her asked the misbehaving student and the rest of the class to arrive at a consensus regarding the problem by suggesting tentative solutions directed the misbehaving student to select a solution and commit to it cited the commitment of the class to helping the misbehaving student in carrying out the solution. | |

Once all the data are described, the teacher quickly moves to get suggestions from both the misbehaving student and the class regarding how to solve the problem with a plan that would be agreeable to everyone. The teacher listens to and records the suggestions, then directs the group to eliminate those which may not be workable or accepted by all.

The misbehaving student selects a plan from one they have all had a part in designing, and commits to implementing the plan. The teacher and the class commit themselves to any actions that will assist the student in achieving success.

The classroom meeting ends with a plan agreeable to all, and committed to by all.

# 11

# Assertive Discipline

## Theory

LEE CANTER, A SPECIALIST IN CHILD GUIDANCE, and Marlene Canter, a learning disabilities specialist, promoted their theory in Assertive Discipline (1976, 1992). Central to the Canter and Canter model is the belief that teachers must develop an assertive attitude and act in an assertive way. This assertive attitude will "empower" teachers to be in charge. They will do so by asserting their right to teach by setting up rules and consequences for obeying and not obeying the rules, and being consistent and persistent in implementing consequences.

According to the Canters, there are three response styles teachers exhibit which have different effects on the tone in the classroom: assertive, hostile, or nonassertive.

1. An assertive teacher knows, states, and protects *reasonable* rights for both herself and the students. Assertive teachers communicate their expectations in a businesslike manner, are consistent in implementing their expectations, and are willing to support their expectations by consequences. The teacher may request input from the students regarding rules and consequences for breaking them, but the ultimate decision regarding both is with the teacher. The Canters believe that *teachers who are assertive get their needs met first*, and in so doing, they are in a better position to help their students. The "help yourself first" analogy is similar to that of

instructions provided by flight attendants just before takeoff. Tauber (1999) paraphrased the instructions by stating, "Should we lose cabin pressure and oxygen will be required, oxygen masks will drop from the ceiling. If you are traveling with small children or elderly companions, first place the mask on yourself, and then attend to the needs of those around you" (p. 71).
2. A hostile teacher uses aggressive, hurtful methods such as threats and sarcasm. It is a case of the teacher against the student. In a hostile environment, students feel insecure, become disrespectful, and are prone to retaliation. Permanent learning cannot take place in this environment because hostile teachers meet their needs first but do not meet the needs of their students.
3. A nonassertive teacher is passive, unfocused, hesitant in demanding expectations from the students, and inconsistent in enforcing standards, thus setting the tone for ineffective leadership. Nonassertive teachers do not meet their needs nor do they meet their students' needs.

In your classroom, Hank and John are talking while Fred is answering a question. Examine the three response styles to this situation, but before you read the different responses, first decide how *you* would respond to Hank and John's behavior.

Assertive teacher response: The teacher walks over to the talking students. If they still continue talking, she says, "Hank and John," she points to the rule on the poster, "the class decided that only one person speaks at a time. Be respectful to Fred, and listen to what he has to say."

Hostile teacher response: "What's the matter with you two? Don't you ever learn? How many times do I have to tell you to stop talking?"

Non-assertive teacher response: "Come on, you guys (a speech "Don't" listed in chapter 2), will you please stop talking? I've asked you so many times."

## Implementation

The Canters claim that the assertive teacher, the one they want to develop, must have a well-designed discipline plan that includes both rules and "limit setting." The rules should be clear, observable, few in number, and posted. A cause-effect set of consequences, both positive and negative, should be arranged in a *hierarchy* to match the degree of student behavior in obeying or not obeying the rules. The plan is then approved by the school after which the plan is taught and practiced in class on the first day of school, sent to parents for their signature, and is consistently enforced on a daily basis.

An important principle in implementing the plan is that it is used *fairly*. In order to do this the teacher must collect data. The effect is that *the data, not the decision of the teacher, will then determine the consequences administered as determined by the discipline plan.*

The Canters have suggested two methods for collecting data, "names on the board" or "marbles in a jar." In the former, when a student misbehaves, her name is written on the board or placed in a grade book or discipline folder. Each time she continues to misbehave, a check mark is added. The consequences of the frequency of the misbehavior are communicated in advance. For example, it may be decided that the name on the board should serve as a warning.

The first check mark next to the name may be staying after class for a specified amount of time, the second check mark gets a longer amount of time. Additional check marks could in addition to the extra time spent include a phone call or e-mail to the parents or a trip to the principal. Once the consequences are implemented, the student begins with a fresh start, thus giving him/her a new opportunity to behave properly.

"Marbles in the jar" is used when the student is behaving, or following a rule. (For older students, Canter (2006) suggests that the teacher should call it "points on the board.") The teacher drops a marble in the jar informing all students that they are accumulating points (marbles) which may be traded in for a reward.

Using rewards for one student or for all students who behave according to the rules is a critical part of the Canters' model. The teacher must determine what every student considers a reward, and then determine a *reinforcement schedule*—how many times the behavior should be demonstrated in order to receive a reward.

Both the "name on the board" and "marbles in the jar" techniques have drawn criticism. The Canters suggest that if these two methods are not acceptable, the teacher should find his own. Other critics oppose the use of rewards (or punishments) in the attempt to achieve desirable behavior (Kohn, 1993, 1996, 2001; Tauber, 2007). They view rewards and praise as calculating, a way for teachers to exercise control over students, and fostering dependency, thereby making it less likely for students to become self-managed.

At the heart of the Canters' model is the concept that the teacher should not accept any excuses from misbehaving students such as coming from an underprivileged or minority background. Misbehaving students should be held accountable because *they* have decided not to obey a rule. The teacher must not waver in delivering a consequence, even when the student who has misbehaved performs better later in the day.

Teachers using Assertive Discipline have several other techniques for delivering their message:

- Voice tone. The message should be delivered in a confident, firm, and businesslike tone. When delivering the message this way, the "broken record" strategy, can be used. The teacher simply repeats persistently the rule or request made of the student until the student complies.
- Gestures. Eye contact, a stare, a raised palm, a finger crossed over the lip, or certain orchestral conducting techniques such as pushing an open hand down convey confidence without interrupting the lesson.
- Using students' names. This technique is an attention-getter, especially when the name is used in context or with the type of voice tone mentioned above.
- "I" messages. You should recall that in both chapters 3 and 8, "I" messages were suggested as effective communicators. Gordon's "I" message (when implementing Teacher Effectiveness Training) had three parts: "When you talk in class" (a description of the misbehavior), "it interrupts my train of thought" (how it tangibly and concretely affected the teacher), and "I get frustrated" (how it made the teacher feel). Gordon then assumes that once this message is communicated, the student will decide if and how to change the behavior.

The Canters have modified Gordon's "I" message to communicate just how the behavior is to be changed. "I feel annoyed" (identification of the feeling) "when you call out answers" (identification of the problem) "and I want you to raise your hand when you have something to say" (state the behavior the teacher wants).

As already described in chapter 3, the Canter "I" message can be expressed to reflect a more contemporary approach by saying, "I feel I'm not doing my job properly [teacher's feeling] when you call out answers [misbehavior], and as the class decided, you should raise your hand if you want to participate in the discussion [behavior agreed to by both class and teacher]."

In the Assertive Discipline model, the assertive teacher is definitely in charge and the class procedures are more structured. However, Assertive Discipline can be made more contemporary in its approach when students are involved in determining rules, as opposed to their being decided solely by the teacher; when students participate in determining both rewards for following and consequences for not following rules; and when the assertive

TABLE 11.1
Coaching Rubric for Assertive Discipline (T)

| Criteria (Descriptors) | Performance Indicators (Examples) |
|---|---|
| The teacher . . . | |
| established a carefully thought-out discipline plan with rules and limits before the opening of school | |
| when possible, established rules with student input on first day of class, but also included those desired by teacher | |
| established with students reasonable rules | |
| established with students clear rules that were simply stated | |
| established with students rules and results with cause-effect relationships | |
| determined with students a hierarchy of positive consequences (rewards) for obeying rules | |
| determined with students a hierarchy of negative consequences for breaking the rules (improper behavior) | |
| determined with students a reinforcement schedule for assigning rewards and consequences. | |
| As soon as mutually agreed upon, the teacher . . . | |
| practiced the rules | |
| submitted the plan for examination and approval by the school administration | |
| communicated plan to parents for signature. | |
| When a student violated a rule, the teacher . . . | |
| repeated request for changing improper behavior no more than three times | |
| communicated request in a firm, confident, businesslike tone | |
| maintained direct eye contact | |
| used appropriate accompanying gestures | |
| incorporated student's name in the request | |
| sent an "I" message (Canter style) | |
| established a record-keeping system for enforcing discipline plan | |
| enforced discipline plan consistently and fairly | |
| allowed every misbehaving student to begin each day anew | |
| "caught" students behaving properly and rewarded them appropriately | |
| avoided "overkill" in distributing rewards. | |

teacher ensures that rules are implemented consistently and takes ultimate responsibility for the class.

The contemporary assertive teacher also fosters mutual respect among all class members and communicates with parents the class expectations. When a student violates a rule, the assertive teacher reminds that student which class-decided rule he is violating or asks the misbehaving student which rule he is violating that shows disrespect for the class.

# 12

# Behavior Modification (Contingency Contracting)

## Theory

B. F. Skinner advanced his theory of behavior modification in *Science and Human Behavior* (1953) and *Beyond Freedom and Dignity* (1971). He was greatly influenced by Pavlov's emphasis on stimulus-response. Pavlov, in a classic experiment, rang a bell just as he was about to feed dogs. After many repetitions of the bell ringing with corresponding feedings, he discovered that dogs would salivate just at the ringing of a bell. Pavlov was able to substitute the bell for the food, the stimulus, which would give the response, salivating.

Skinner applied stimulus-response theory to humans. Humans, just as other animals, respond to stimuli within their environment. The inner rational person described by Carl Rogers (1969, 1971, 1981), who influenced Gordon in his development of Teacher Effectiveness Training (chapter 8), does not exist in the world of the behaviorist. As a result, rational behavior on the part of the student occurs because parents, teachers, or other adults have either rewarded that behavior or have ignored or punished irrational behavior.

Skinnerians believe that the key to changing misbehavior is changing the student's environment. Students will seek experiences in the environment that are pleasurable and rewarding and avoid those that are not. Behaviorists are not concerned with discovering the causes of students' problems. Providing teachers with information regarding the students' past experiences such as being deprived financially or academically or suffering abuse, is, according to behaviorists, not helpful in dealing with the present, the here and now.

Classroom time constraints also do not allow the teacher to discuss the students' inner feelings or have the students come up with their own solutions to problems. All the teacher can do is rearrange the classroom environment to help the student reverse the misbehavior. However, in so doing, the teacher first discusses the misbehavior with the student and then develops with him or her a system (contract) for eliminating the inappropriate behavior.

This approach is contemporary when the teacher arranges a supportive classroom environment and seeks the student's input into solving the behavior problem. Behaviorists believe that all behavior, both appropriate and inappropriate, is learned. When a student behaves appropriately or inappropriately, either of these kinds of behavior results in a consequence. The consequences fall into four categories:

1. Introducing a reward (*positive reinforcement*);
2. Removing a reward (*extinction*), or removing the student physically from the reward (time out);
3. Introducing a punishment (an undesirable or *aversive stimulus*);
4. Removing punishment (*negative reinforcement*).

How often a particular behavior occurs depends (is contingent) upon the nature of the consequences occurring immediately after the behavior. Rewarding a behavior and removing negative reinforcement, 1 and 4 above, tend to strengthen behavior and, therefore, its frequency. Removing a reward from the student or introducing punishment, 2 and 3 above, are inclined to weaken the behavior and, therefore, decrease its frequency.

Keep in mind that according to the theory, consequence number 3 above, introducing a punishment, and consequence number 4, negative reinforcement, are *not* the same. Reinforcement, whether it be positive or negative, strengthens behavior, and punishment weakens (suppresses) behavior.

In applying the four categories of consequences, timing and frequency of punishment and reinforcement are critical. The behavior the teacher desires to encourage should be reinforced immediately after it is displayed or it will tend to become weakened; behavior the teacher desires to discourage should be punished immediately after it is displayed or it will tend to become strengthened. In terms of frequency, reinforcement that occurs each time the behavior is displayed leads to learning that behavior more rapidly. Punishing a behavior each time it occurs causes that behavior to be suppressed more quickly.

Once the behavior is learned, it may be reinforced more effectively using intermittent reinforcement. Intermittent reinforcement may be applied by using an *interval schedule* or a *ratio schedule*. Using an interval schedule, the teacher reinforces the behavior after a specific *amount of time,* for example, an hour, a morning, a day. An interval schedule is more effective for maintaining *consistent* behavior.

Using a ratio schedule, the teacher reinforces the behavior after it has been displayed a specific *number of times*, for example, every five times. A ratio schedule is more effective in producing a *higher frequency* of the behavior.

Rewarding and punishing all behavior indiscriminately will lead to negative consequences. Rewarding an undesirable behavior will tend to increase its frequency, for example, calling on a student who calls out. Punishing desirable behavior will tend to decrease its frequency, for example, ignoring a student who always volunteers.

## Implementation

The behavior modification (contingency contracting) model has four basic steps:

1. Identifying the target behavior—the problem behavior to be changed or modified;
2. Recording the frequency of the target behavior;
3. Changing the target behavior by reinforcing a desired behavior with a reward;
4. Selecting the reward.

### Types of Reinforcers (Rewards)

A reinforcer (reward) used in behavior modification should be personal. One student's reward may not be one valued by another. The reward selected should be the one having the greatest potential to increase the frequency of the reinforced behavior.

In general there are two types of reinforcers: innate, or *primary reinforcers*; and learned, or *conditioned reinforcers*. Primary (innate) reinforcers are our basic needs, such as water, food, and shelter. Conditioned (learned) reinforcers include:

a. Social reinforcers—any verbal or nonverbal approval such as praise, a smile, wink, pat on the head, or a nod.
b. Privilege reinforcers—being a monitor, using the computer, exemption from a test, using a game or simulation.
c. Graphic reinforcers—pictures or numerals stamped on papers or on the hand.

d. Tangible reinforcers—actual objects such as badges, books, certificates, and stickers, or edibles such as a slice of pizza, cookies, or candy.
e. Token reinforcers—an accumulated number of points, stars, script, or tickets that can be traded or cashed in for a tangible reinforcer such as a ticket to a movie, lunch at Burger King, or a trip to a concert.

Contingency Contracting is more contemporary in nature when the teacher arranges a supportive classroom environment and seeks the student's input into solving his or her behavior problem. The student identifies the target behavior, and must agree that this behavior should be eliminated. The student is then *personally* involved in selecting the reward(s) and in determining the reinforcement schedule. Thus, self-management of behavior is emphasized. The class encourages the student in eliminating the undesirable behavior.

**TABLE 12.1**
**Coaching Rubric for Behavior Modification (Contingency Contracting) [T]**

| Criteria (Descriptors) | Performance Indicators (Examples) |
|---|---|
| The teacher . . . | |
| explained to the student the purpose of meeting with him/her | |
| asked the student to state the target behavior (the one to be eliminated) | |
| described in detail the new behavior to be achieved | |
| asked the student to put in her own words the new behavior to be achieved | |
| ensured that the student agreed that the new behavior should be achieved. | |
| If the student did not agree, the teacher . . . | |
| ended the meeting on pleasant terms. | |
| If the student did agree, the teacher . . . | |
| asked what reinforcers (activities, objects, privileges) she would like | |
| negotiated the ratio of behavior to reinforcement | |
| indicated the time frame for the demonstration of the new behavior | |
| discussed and negotiated how progress in demonstrating the new behavior will be evaluated | |
| negotiated the delivery of the reinforcement | |
| made an appointment for a progress report | |
| put in writing the terms of the agreement | |
| signed agreement and had the student sign also | |
| praised the student for her efforts. | |

In the beginning of part 2 you were asked to submit to a philosophy/personality belief check. Now that you have reviewed the strategies presented in this section, determine which strategies are most consistent and compatible with your beliefs. Do you think that only one strategy should be adopted and implemented consistently, or that you can use parts from several strategies in your class? Why did you make your choice?

Kohn (1996) believes that democratic communities should be established in classrooms instead of traditional classroom management systems that have created unthinking, compliant students. He has offered his vision for classroom management.

It includes: encouraging students with the teacher's guidance to develop appropriate behavior for themselves; having students participate in making daily decisions regarding their learning processes; conducting classroom meetings periodically for students to vent their feelings and discuss classroom issues and problems within a democratic setting; providing opportunities for students to determine classroom standards of behavior; and creating a positive, safe environment that allows full student participation without the fear of ridicule and negative feedback.

Which guidelines in part 1 and strategies in part 2 of this book support Kohn's vision and which do not?

## Part 2 Summary

Teacher Effectiveness Training fosters open communication between teacher and student. This communication must not be impeded through roadblocks such as ordering, criticizing, agreeing, or judging because they prevent a student from solving his own problem(s). When there is a problem in the classroom, the teacher must first decide who owns the problem—the student, the teacher, or both.

If the student owns the problem, he is the only one affected by it. In this case the teacher communicates through critical listening, door openers, and active listening. If the teacher owns the problem, one that concretely affects her, the teacher sends an "I" message (Gordon-style). If both student and teacher own the problem, the teacher employs the "no-lose" method in which the problem is defined and tentative solutions are generated and evaluated. Then one or more solutions are selected, implemented, and evaluated for efficacy.

When implementing Social Discipline, the teacher must first determine the student's faulty goal (attention, power, revenge, helplessness). This determination is accomplished by the teacher's asking four internal questions regarding how the student's behavior manifesting the faulty goal makes the teacher feel (annoyed, intimidated, hurt, incapable).

The teacher then verifies the faulty goal by asking external questions while simultaneously looking for the student's reaction reflex in the response. Once the faulty goal has been confirmed, the teacher imposes natural/logical consequences associated with any misbehavior the student displays relevant to the goal.

The Reality Therapy strategy holds students accountable for their own behavior by accepting the consequences of that behavior, and committing themselves to becoming more responsible toward others. To nurture this responsibility the teacher creates a warm and caring relationship with the misbehaving student, has the student identify her own misbehavior, and has the student verbalize the relationship between the misbehavior and its result.

The student then designs a plan to correct the misbehavior and signs a formal agreement to implement the plan. If the plan is violated, logical consequences are applied. If necessary, a new plan is designed.

The Classroom Meeting, an application of Reality Therapy, is implemented when a problem affects the whole class. The meeting may be open-ended for exploring ideas or imaginary problems, educational/diagnostic for assisting the teacher in making curriculum and/or instructional decisions, or problem solving for making a decision that affects all students, in particular, solving a specific behavior problem of one student. The purpose of the meeting then becomes helping this student behave in a more appropriate way.

During the classroom meeting, the students sit in a circle and each class member including the teacher individually faces the misbehaving student in a nonconfrontational and courteous way and specifies what the misbehavior was, and how it affected him or her personally. The misbehaving student then describes what others in the class have done to him. When all the information is gathered, the misbehaving student and class together offer alternative plans to solve the problem. The misbehaving student selects one of the plans and everyone in the class commits to supporting the misbehaving student in implementing the plan successfully.

When using Assertive Discipline, a teacher takes the lead in dealing with the class. An assertive teacher provides reasonable rights for both himself and the students, is businesslike and consistent in implementing expectations, and supports expectations with consequences. The disciplinary plan includes rules and limit setting with a cause-effect set of positive consequences (rewards) for complying with the rules, and negative consequences for disregarding them.

The positive and negative consequences are published in advance along with the number of times they must occur to receive the reward or consequence. In order to implement the discipline plan fairly, the teacher collects data.

The first data collection method is "names on the board"—the listing of the name of any misbehaving student with added checkmarks for repeated offenses. The second method is "marbles in a jar" in which a marble is dropped into a jar when students are behaving so that the marbles can be exchanged for a reward.

The assertive teacher accepts no excuses for misbehavior. Besides delivering negative consequences, the teacher addresses misbehavior first through voice tone, gestures, using the student's name, and "I" messages (Canter-style).

Behavior Modification (Contingency Contracting) is based on stimulus-response theory. Behaviorists believe that rational student behavior occurs because that behavior was rewarded by teachers (parents, other adults) or ignored or punished by them. To change misbehavior, the student's environment must be altered so that the student will seek pleasurable (rewarding) experiences and avoid unpleasant ones.

Behaviorists propose that all behavior is learned and results in a consequence. Consequences that strengthen behavior are introducing a reward (positive reinforcement) and removing punishment (negative reinforcement). Consequences that weaken behavior are removing a reward (extinction) and introducing punishment (an undesirable stimulus). Timing and frequency of consequences are critical.

Learned behavior may be strengthened by applying an interval schedule, in which the behavior is reinforced after it is displayed a specified *amount* of time, or a ratio schedule in which the exhibited behavior is reinforced after it occurs a specific *number* of times.

When implementing Behavior Modification, the target behavior (behavior to be changed) is identified; the frequency of the target behavior is recorded; that target behavior is changed by rewarding a desired behavior; and a reward is selected. There are two kinds of reinforcers: primary (innate) reinforcers such as water, food, and shelter, and learned (conditioned) reinforcers such as social, privilege, graphic, tangible, or token.

# References

Ashcraft, M. (2002). *Cognition*, 3rd ed. Upper Saddle River, NJ: Prentice Hall.
Beane, A. L. (1999). *The bully free classroom: Over 100 tips and strategies for teachers K–8.* Minneapolis, MN: Free Spirit Publishing.
Bowers, C., & Flinders, D. (1991). *Culturally responsive teaching and supervision: A handbook for staff development.* New York: Teachers College Press.
Boynton, M., & Boynton, C. (2005). *The educator's guide to preventing and solving discipline problems.* Alexandria, VA: Association for Supervision and Curriculum Development.
Brookhart, S. M. (2004). *Grading.* Upper Saddle River, NJ: Pearson Education.
Brooks, D. (2011). *The social animal: The hidden sources of love, character, and achievement.* New York: Random House.
Brophy, J. (1996). *Teaching problem students.* New York: Guilford.
Brophy, J., & Evertson, C. (1976). *Learning from teaching: A developmental perspective.* Boston: Allyn & Bacon.
Cangelosi, J. (2004). *Classroom management strategies: Gaining and maintaining students' cooperation,* 5th ed. Hoboken, NJ: Wiley.
Cangelosi, J. (2008). *Classroom management strategies: Gaining and maintaining students' cooperation,* 6th ed. Hoboken, NJ: Wiley.
Canter, L. (2006). *Classroom management for academic success.* Bloomington, IN: Solution Tree.
Canter, L., & Canter, M. (1976). *Assertive discipline: A take-charge approach for today's educator.* Seal Beach, CA: Canter & Associates.
Canter, L., & Canter, M. (1992). *Assertive discipline.* Santa Monica, CA: Canter & Associates.
Canter, L., & Canter, M. (2001). *Assertive discipline: Positive behavior management for today's classrooms,* 3rd ed. Santa Monica, CA: Canter & Associates.

Churchward, B. (2009). *Discipline by design.* http://honorlevel.com.
Cotton, K. (1990). *School management series. Close-up #9: Schoolwide and classroom discipline.* Portland, OR: Northwest Regional Educational Laboratory.
Cotton, K. (2000). *The schooling practices that matter most.* Alexandria, VA: Association for Supervision and Curriculum Development.
Cummings, C. (2000). *Winning strategies for classroom management.* Alexandria, VA: Association for Supervision and Curriculum Development.
Curwin, R., & Mendler, A. (1999). *Discipline with dignity,* 2nd ed. Alexandria, VA: Association for Supervision and Curriculum Development.
Curwin, R., Mendler, A., & Mendler, B. (2008). *Discipline with dignity: New challenges, new solutions,* 3rd ed. Alexandria, VA: Association for Supervision and Curriculum Development.
Damani, B. (2011, February). Creating win-win classrooms. *Education Update,* 53(2), Alexandria, VA: Association for Supervision and Curriculum Development.
Danielson, C. (2007). *Enhancing professional practice: A framework for teaching,* 2nd ed. Alexandria, VA: Association for Supervision and Curriculum Development.
Danielson, C., & McGreal, T. (2000). *Teacher evaluation to enhance professional practice.* Alexandria, VA: Association for Supervision and Curriculum Development.
Delpit, L. (1995). *Other people's children: Cultural conflict in the classroom.* New York: The New Press.
Dreikurs, R. (1968). *Psychology in the classroom: A manual for teachers,* 2nd ed. New York: Harper & Row.
Dreikurs, R. (1998). *Maintaining sanity in the classroom: Classroom management techniques,* 2nd ed. Washington, DC: Accelerated Development.
Emmer, E., Evertson, C., & Worsham, M. (2003a). *Classroom management for elementary teachers,* 6th ed. Boston: Allyn & Bacon.
Emmer, E., Evertson, C., & Worsham, M. (2003b). *Classroom management for secondary teachers,* 6th ed. Boston: Allyn & Bacon.
Engel, S., & Sandstrom, M. (2010, July 22). There's only one way to stop a bully. *New York Times,* A23.
Evertson, C., & Weinstein, C. (Eds.) (2006). *Handbook of classroom management: Research, practice, and contemporary issues.* Mahwah, NJ: Erlbaum.
Fay, J., & Funk, D. (1995). *Teaching with love and logic.* Golden, CO: Love & Logic Press.
Franklin, J. (2006, March). The essential ounce of prevention: Effective classroom Management means more than intervention. *Education Update,* 48(3), 3–8, Association for Supervision and Curriculum Development.
Gammill, A. (2010, May 21). IPS teacher goes from mutiny to best in class. Indystar.com.
George, C. (2008, December 3). Teaching secrets: Taming the dragon of classroom chaos. www.edweek.org.
Gewertz, C. (2008, October 15). States press ahead on "21st-century skills," *Education Week,* 28(8), 21–23.
Glasser, W. (1969). *Schools without failure.* New York: Harper & Row.
Glasser, W. (1975). *Reality therapy: A new approach to psychiatry.* New York: Harper & Row.

Glasser, W. (1986). *Control theory in the classroom.* New York: Harper & Row.
Glasser W. (1992). *The quality school: Managing students without coercion*, 2nd ed. New York: HarperCollins.
Goleman, D. (1998). *Working with emotional intelligence.* New York: Bantam Books.
Good, T., & Brophy, J. (1974). Changing teacher and student behavior: An empirical investigation. *Journal of Educational Psychology*, 66, 390–405.
Good, T., & Brophy, J. (2003). *Looking in classrooms*, 9th ed. Boston: Allyn & Bacon.
Gootman, M. (1997). *The caring teacher's guide to discipline.* Thousand Oaks, CA: Corwin Press.
Gordon, T. (1970). *Parent effectiveness training.* New York: Peter H. Weyden.
Gordon, T. (1974). *Teacher effectiveness training.* New York: Peter H. Weyden.
Gordon, T. (1977). *Leader effectiveness training.* New York: Peter H. Weyden.
Haber, J. (2007). *Bullyproof your child for life: Protect your child from teasing, taunting, and bullying for good.* New York: Penguin/Perigee.
Hall, E. (1977). *Beyond culture.* Garden City, NY: Anchor.
Hanson, J. R. (1998). *Classroom management: An ASCD professional inquiry kit.* Alexandria, VA: Association for Supervision and Curriculum Development.
Hayes, S., Rosenfarb, I., Wulfert, E., Munt, E., Korn, Z., & Zettle, R. (1985). Self-reinforcement effects: An artifact of social standard setting? *Journal of Applied Behavioral Analysis*, 18, 201–14.
Hook, C., & Rosenshine, B. (1979). Accuracy of teacher reports of their classroom behavior. *Review of Educational Research*, 49, 1–12.
Hoover, J., & Oliver, R. (1996). *The bullying prevention handbook: A guide for principals, teachers, and counselors.* Bloomington, IN: National Educational Service.
Hunter, R. (2004). *Madeline Hunter's mastery teaching: Increasing instructional effectiveness in elementary and secondary schools*, updated edition. Thousand Oaks, CA: Corwin Press.
Jensen, E. (1998). *Teaching with the brain in mind.* Alexandria, VA: Association for Supervision and Curriculum Development.
Jensen, E. (2005). *Teaching with the brain in mind*, 2nd ed. Alexandria, VA: Association for Supervision and Curriculum Development.
Johns, B., & Carr, V. (1995). *Techniques for managing verbally and physically aggressive students.* Columbia, MO: Hawthorne Educational Services.
Jones, F. H. (1979). The gentle art of classroom discipline. *National Elementary Principal*, 58(4), 26–32.
Jones, F. H. (1987). *Positive classroom discipline.* New York: McGraw-Hill.
Jones, F. H. (2000). *Tools for teaching.* Santa Cruz, CA: Fred H. Jones & Associates.
Jones, V. F., & Jones, L. S. (2003). *Comprehensive classroom management: Creating communities of support and solving problems*, 7th ed. Boston: Allyn & Bacon.
Joyce, B., & Showers, B. (1995). *Student achievement through staff development*, 2nd ed. New York: Longman.
Joyce, B, & Showers, B. (2002). *Student achievement through staff development*, 3rd ed. Alexandria, VA: Association for Supervision and Curriculum Development.
Juvonen, J., Graham, S., & Schuster, M. (2003). Bullying among young adolescents: The strong, the weak, and the troubled. *Pediatrics*, 112, 1231–37.

Karweit, N. (1988). Time on task: The second time around. *NASSP Bulletin*, 72(505), 31–39.

Kaufman, D., & Moss, D. (2010, April). A new look at preservice teachers' conceptions of classroom management and organization: Uncovering complexity and dissonance. *The Teacher Educator*, 45(2), 118–36.

Kohlberg, L. (1981). *The philosophy of moral development.* New York: Harper and Row.

Kohn, A. (1993). *Punished by rewards.* Boston: Houghton Mifflin.

Kohn, A. (1996). *Beyond discipline: From compliance to community.* Alexandria, VA: Association for Supervision and Curriculum Development.

Kohn, A. (2001, September). Five reasons to stop saying "good job." *Young Children*, http://www.alfiekohn.org.

Kohn, A. (2003, March). Almost there, but not quite. *Educational Leadership*, 58(3), 20–24.

Kohn, A. (2005, May 23). Atrocious advice from "supernanny." *Nation.* http://alfiekohn.org.

Kohn, A. (2007, September 19). Against "competitiveness": Why good teachers aren't thinking about the global economy. *Education Week*, 27(4), 1–32.

Kohn, A. (2008). Why self-discipline is overrated: The (troubling) theory and practice of control from within. *Phi Delta Kappan*, 90(3), 168–76.

Kottler, J. A., Zehm, S. J., & Kottler, E. (2005). *On becoming a teacher: The human dimension*, 3rd ed. Thousand Oaks, CA: Corwin Press.

Kounin, J. S. (1970). *Discipline and group management in classrooms.* New York: Holt, Rinehart, & Winston.

Lazear, D. (1998). *The rubrics way: Using MI to assess understanding.* Tuscon, AZ: Zephyr Press.

Long, J., & Frye, V. (1985). *Making it till Friday: A guide to successful classroom management*, 3rd ed. Princeton, NJ: Princeton Book Company.

Mace, F., Belfiore, P. & Hutchinson, J. (2001). Operant theory and research on self-regulation. In B. Zimmerman & D. Schunk (eds.), *Self-regulated learning and academic achievement: Theoretical perspectives*, 2nd ed. Mahwah, NJ: Erlbaum.

MacKenzie, R. (1996). *Setting limits in the classroom: How to move beyond the classroom dance of discipline.* Roseville, CA: Prima.

Marzano, R. (2003a). *What works in schools: Translating research into action.* Alexandria, VA: Association for Supervision and Curriculum Development.

Marzano, R. (2003b). *Classroom management that works.* Alexandria, VA: Association for Supervision and Curriculum Development.

Marzano, R. (2007). *The art and science of teaching: A comprehensive framework for effective instruction.* Alexandria, VA: Association for Supervision and Curriculum Development.

McGee, K. (2008). How cultural differences may affect student performance. *Great Schools.* http://www.greatschools.net.

McLeod, J., Fisher, J., & Hoover, G. (2003). *The key elements of classroom management: Managing time and space, student behavior, and instructional strategies.* Alexandria, VA: Association for Supervision and Curriculum Development.

McNeil, M. (2009, July 15). Bullying a top concern for new safe-schools chief. *Education Week*, (28)36, 15–18.
National Education Association (n.d.). *Discipline checklist: Advice from 60 successful teachers.* NEA Professional Library, http://www/nea.org/classmanagement/transitions.
National Education Association (2009). (http://www.nea.org/home/ToolsAndIdeas.html)
Orloff, S. (2008). The whole child. *Exceptional Parent*, 38(5), 48–49.
Osher, D., Bear, G., Sprague, J., & Doyle, W. (2010). How can we improve school discipline? *Educational Researcher*, 39(1), 48–58.
Peterson, P. (2010, April 21). Finding the student's "price point." *Education Week*, 29(29), 40.
Pianta, R. (2007, November 6). Measure actual classroom teaching. *Education Week*, http://www.edweek.org/ew/articles/2007/11/07/11pianta.
Piaget, J. (1954). The construction of reality in the child, M. Cook, trans. New York: Basic Books.
Piaget, J. (1963). *Origins of intelligence in children.* New York: Norton.
Piaget, J. (1964). Development and learning. In R. Ripple & V. Rockcastle (eds.), *Piaget rediscovered* (pp. 7–20). Ithaca, NY: Cornell University Press.
Pintrich, P., & Schunk, D. (2002). *Motivation in education: Theory, research, and applications*, 2nd ed. Upper Saddle River, NJ: Merrill/Prentice Hall.
Ratzel, M. (2010, May 5). Teaching secrets: 10 to-dos for new teachers. http://www.edweek.org/tm/articles/2010/05/05/tln_ratzel_newteachertodos.html
Reiman, A., & Thies-Sprinthall, L. (1998). *Mentoring and supervision for teacher development.* New York: Longman.
Rigsbee, C. (2008, January). Positively teaching. *Teacher Magazine.* http://www.teachermagazine.org/tm/articles/2008/01/30/20tln_rigsbee_web.h19.html
Rodkin, P., Farmer, T., Pearl, R, & VanAcker, R. (2000). Heterogeneity of popular boys: Antisocial and prosocial configurations. *Developmental Psychology*, (36), 14–24.
Rogers, C. (1969). *Freedom to learn.* Columbus, OH: Charles E. Merrill.
Rogers, C. (1971). *Client-centered therapy.* Boston: Houghton Mifflin.
Rogers, C. (1981). *A way of being.* Boston: Houghton Mifflin.
Rosenshine, B. (1979). Content, time, and direct instruction. In P. L. Peterson and H. J. Walberg (eds.), *Research on teaching: Concepts, findings, and implications.* Berkeley, CA: McCutchan.
Ryan, K., Cooper, J., & Tauer, S. (2008). *Teaching for student learning: Becoming a master teacher.* Boston: Houghton Mifflin.
Sadker, M., & Sadker, D. (1994). *Failing at fairness: How America's schools cheat girls.* New York: Scribner.
Schmid, R. (2008, November 21). Messy neighborhoods affect behavior, study finds. *The Journal News*, B4.
Scollon, R. (1985). The machine stops: Silence in the metaphor of malfunction. In D. Tannen & M. Saville-Troike (eds.), *Perspectives on Silence.* Norwood, NJ: Ablex.
Secretary's Commission on Achieving Necessary Skills (1991). *What work requires of schools: A SCANS report for America 2000.* Washington, D.C.: U.S. Department of Labor.

Shah, N. (2011a, February 8). Study disputes myth of school bullies' social status. *Education Week*, 30(21) 1–12.

Shah, N. (2011b, March 30). Anonymous bullying on social network seeps into schools. *Education Week*, 30(27).

Shulkind, S. (2008, April 28). Reframing bullying in middle schools. *Teacher Magazine*. http://www.teacher magazine.org/tm/articles/2008/04/28/tm_shulkind.

Skinner, B. F. (1953). *Science and human behavior*. Boston: Houghton Mifflin.

Skinner, B. F. (1971). *Beyond freedom and dignity*. New York: Alfred E. Knopf.

Smart J., & Igo, L. (2010, June). A grounded theory of behavior management selection, implementation, and perceived effectiveness reported by first-year elementary teachers. *Elementary School Journal*, 110(4) 567–84.

Starr, L. (2003). Are you a bully? *Education World*. http://www.educationworld.com/a_issues/starr/starr056.shtml.

Stefanou, C., Perencevich, K., DiCintio, M., & Turner, J. (2004). Supporting autonomy in the classroom: Ways teachers encourage student decision making and ownership. *Educational Psychologist*, 39(2), 97–110.

Steinberg, L. (1996). *Beyond the classroom: Why school reform has failed and what parents need to do*. New York: Simon & Schuster.

Sternberg, D. (2010, April 16). Training teacher's pe(s)ts. *New York Times*, Education Life, p. 18.

Sylwester, R. (2000, November). Unconscious emotions, conscious feelings. *Educational Leadership*, 58(3), 20–24.

Tate, M. (2007). *Shouting won't grow dendrites: 20 techniques for managing a brain-compatible classroom*. Thousand Oaks, CA: Corwin Press.

Tauber, R. (1999). *Classroom management: Sound theory and effective practice*, 3rd ed. Westport, CT: Bergin & Garvey.

Tauber, R. (2007). *Classroom management: Sound theory and effective practice*, 4th ed. Portsmouth, NH: Praeger.

Tedrow, M. (2008, May 28). Best practices: The miracle of choices. *Teacher Magazine*. http://www.edweek.org/tm/articles/2008/05/28/35tln_tedrow.h19.html.

Tomlinson, C. (2001). *How to differentiate instruction in mixed-ability classrooms*, 2nd ed. Alexandria, VA: Association for Supervision and Curriculum Development.

University of Florida (2008, April 23). Social form of bullying linked to depression, anxiety in adults. *Science Daily*. Retrieved April 25 from http://www.sciencedaily.com/releases/2008/04/080422143529.htm.

Viadero, D. (2010, May 19). Study sees broad view of bullying culture. *Education Week*, 29(32), 1, 18–29.

Vygotsky, L. (1997). *Educational psychology*, R. Silverman, trans. Boca Raton, FL: St. Lucie.

Walker, H., Ramsey, E., & Gresham, F. (2004). *Antisocial behavior in school: Evidence-based practices*, 2nd ed. Belmont, CA: Wadsworth/Thomson.

Wang, M., Haertel, G., & Walberg, H. (1993). Toward a knowledge base for school learning. *Review of Educational Research*, 63(3), 249–94.

Washburn, S., Stowe, K., Cole, C, & Robinson, J. (2007, Fall). Improving school climate and student behavior: A new paradigm for Indiana Schools. Educational Policy Brief, *Center for Evaluation and Educational Policy*, 5(9).

West, P. (2009, June 29). Cyber bullying affects one in 10 students. *HealthDay Reporter.*

Wiggins, G. (2005). *Educative assessment,* 2nd ed. Alexandria, VA: Association for Supervision and Curriculum Development.

Wolfe, P. (2001). *Brain matters: Translating research into classroom practice.* Alexandria, VA: Association for Supervision and Curriculum Development.

Wolfgang, C. (1999). *Solving discipline problems: Methods and models for today's teachers,* 4th ed. Boston: Allyn & Bacon.

Wolfgang, C. (2005). *Solving discipline and classroom management problems: Methods and models for today's teachers,* 6th ed., Hoboken, NJ: Wiley.

Wolk, S. (2008, September). Joy in school. *Educational Leadership,* 60(1), 8–15.

Wong, H., & Wong, R. (1998). *The first days of school.* Mountain View, CA: Harry K. Wong Publications.

Wong, H., & Wong, R. (2004). *The first days of school: How to be an effective teacher,* 3rd ed. Mountain View, CA: Harry K. Wong Publications.

Wong, H., & Wong, R. (2005, September). *Effective teaching.* www.teachers.net/gazette.

Woolfolk, A. (2004). *Educational psychology,* 9th ed. Boston: Allyn & Bacon.

Woolfolk, A. (2008). *Educational psychology,* 10th ed. Boston: Pearson

Worley, D. (2006, June 10). Gangs spread in the burbs. *Journal News,* 10A.

# About the Author

**Marie Pagliaro** is currently a professional development consultant. She was a full professor and director of the Teacher Education Division at Dominican College, chair of the Education Department at Marymount College, a supervisor of student teachers at Lehman College of the City University of New York, and chair of the Science Department and teacher of chemistry, general science, and mathematics in the Yonkers Public Schools. She received her PhD in curriculum and teaching from Fordham University.

www.ingramcontent.com/pod-product-compliance
Lightning Source LLC
Chambersburg PA
CBHW021852300426
44115CB00005B/132